F
II
YO
TO

BOOKS BY ALFRED TACK

HOW TO SUCCEED IN SELLING

HOW TO OVERCOME NERVOUS TENSION
AND SPEAK WELL IN PUBLIC

1 000 WAYS TO INCREASE YOUR SALES

HOW TO SUCCEED AS A SALES MANAGER

HOW TO INCREASE SALES BY TELEPHONE

BUILDING, TRAINING AND MOTIVATING
A SALES FORCE

MARKETING: THE SALES MANAGER'S ROLE

HOW TO INCREASE YOUR SALES TO INDUSTRY

Alfred Tack

An imprint of William Heinemann Ltd

Published by Cedar
an imprint of
William Heinemann Limited
Michelin House, 81 Fulham Road, London SW3 6RB

LONDON MELBOURNE AUCKLAND

First published as a hardback 1975
Published as a Cedar book 1980
Second impression 1984
Third impression 1988
Fourth impression 1989

0 434 11126 0

Printed and bound in Great Britain by
Cox & Wyman Ltd, Reading

Contents

Chapter		Page
1	The Importance of the Industrial Salesman	7
2	Salesmanship is Influencing Minds	14
3	Selling by Objectives	22
4	Identifying the Buyer	26
5	Buyer Analysis	42
6	Buyer Motivation	56
7	Obtaining the Interview	70
8	Planning the Call	82
9	Offer Analysis	89
10	The ABC of Selling	110
11	The Opening . . . Getting the Attention of the Buyer	122
12	Closing the Sale	145
13	Overcoming Objections	158
14	Selling through Specifying Authorities	178
15	Territory Planning and Management	187
16	The Professional Salesman	205

I

The Importance of the Industrial Salesman

We walked into Hargreaves' factory reception hall together; he was a management consultant working on an assignment, and I was hoping to close an order. The consultant was waved through, but before I could tell the commissionaire of my appointment, the works director, Mr Fisher, appeared and, seeing me called out, 'I won't keep you a few minutes, Mr Tack, I've made out the order but I want to talk to you about delivery.' The consultant stopped in his stride, turned, smiled and said, 'That's an easy one. I bet you wish they were all like that!'

He walked on, never to learn the truth. I had been chasing that order for six months; six months of hard labour. When I first heard of the inquiry I called to see Mr Fisher, who referred me to the architect responsible for building the factory extension. On hearing the architect's name I knew I had a problem. He had always looked most favourably on the systems marketed by our biggest competitor. Soon, I was trying every device known to me at that time to obtain an interview with that architect—'phone calls, letters, personal calls—I was always fobbed off by one of his juniors.

One day I learned that the ventilation system of our competitors had been specified. Back I went to the architect and almost camped in his waiting-room. One day he brushed past me with a wave of his hand, explaining over his shoulder that he had an appointment.

Disconsolately I followed him out. About to get into my car, I heard a starter motor whirring. The architect's car wouldn't start.

You've guessed what happened. I gave him a lift in my car, and at the end of the journey, just as I was about to broach the subject of Hargreaves' building extension he said, 'Come and see me tomorrow morning at eleven o'clock.'

Next day he listened to me and later, added our name as a specifying company for that contract.

Luck? I suppose every salesman can tell a similar story, but persistence must not be mistaken for luck. Fortunately, I knew the contractor well, and following telephone and personal calls, he agreed to wait for our quotation. Later, this was accepted.

Then what happened in this selling saga? The Board at Hargreaves' decided that there would have to be economies—a credit squeeze had started. Having just taken over a small firm of building contractors they decided to use their own resources to build the extension, so I had to start all over again, selling this time to Mr Fisher and Hargreaves' builders.

Eventually, I got the order. Do you remember the words of the consultant accompanying me into the factory?

'That's an easy one.'

Easy? It was a damned near-run thing, as Wellington once said. And I haven't even mentioned the time spent by draughtsmen and ventilation engineers in preparing the quotations, the seemingly endless journeys—letters—arguments with our own designers.

The consultant, of course, was only making a passing remark, but very few people appreciate the background to industrial selling. They only know of the tip of the iceberg—the person-to-person interview.

The factory extension episode occurred many years ago, but only recently we had yet another example of the lack of appreciation of what industrial selling entails.

We were approached by a film director who wanted to make a TV documentary on salesmanship.

When asked what type of selling he visualised he conjured up a picture of three men: a salesman of detergents, unloved perhaps because of the manner in which detergents are advertised and promoted; a speciality salesman, strongly selling encyclopaedias, cold store units, or double glazing to householders; and an elderly, wise salesman, selling to friendly store buyers—a salesman of charm and integrity, to prove that salesmanship is a worthwhile career. He had not considered introducing a salesman selling to industry because he believed that they were in the minority and would not, therefore, typify the modern salesman at work.

To him, most salesmen sold either to shops or to house-holders—a view held by many people. The TV film producer could hardly credit the truth when he learned that the greatest volume of sales was made by men selling to industry. He felt that our claim was wrong and said, 'Just think of all the thousands of salesmen selling to shops and stores every day.' He changed his mind when we were able to provide him with some facts.

In 1973 the Defence Budget was £1,460 million, which, as the *Daily Telegraph* stated in April of that year, *will result in immense orders being placed through contractors and sub-contractors and will touch almost every industrial group in the country.*

And every one of those suppliers employs salesmen.

The British Leyland Motor Corporation uses some three-and-a-half thousand different suppliers, while Ford spends about £180 millions a year on components, and it is industrial salesmen who sell to the B.L.M.C. and Ford. The overall turnover in industrial sales is nearly five times greater than the combined sales of all consumer goods. When we mentioned to the TV producer the purchasing power of the local authorities and the buying potential of companies in electronics, aircraft and shipping, his thoughts turned immediately to making a film documentary on industrial selling.

We pointed out the difficulty of portraying an industrial salesman at work. What TV audience would want to see weeks of planning, lengthy discussions about phased delivery, researchers at work, visits with a buyer to site, persuading draughtsmen to get drawings finished on time, pleading with head office to hurry through quotations, consulting with experts, phoning—phoning—phoning. And all this before the day of decision.

There was not enough viewer appeal in this aspect of selling for our producer. He explained that he wanted to depict the human side of selling—but he never got around to explaining

what he really meant by that. So that particular documentary
was never made.

The fact is that industrial selling is different from all other
forms of salesmanship, not only because of the time factor
(interviews over long periods, negotiations taking months, etc.),
but for two other main reasons:

1. The importance of industrial selling to the community.
2. The effect his qualifications can have on the salesman.

The Importance of Industrial Selling to the Community

Try to imagine the almost impossible—a salesman's strike
lasting about twelve months, with pickets making it extremely
difficult for anyone to contact buyers.

How would this strike affect buyers and suppliers?

In the consumer field companies could still sell at possibly a
75% level by increased advertising, telephoning, writing
letters. . . .

In the consumer durable field, lack of salesmen would mean
that shop and store assistants would not be kept up to date on
the technical improvements, in, for example, washing machines,
refrigerators, or television sets. Also, very few new models could
be introduced. Advertising would be intensified to teach, inform,
and sell, but in this area, sales would fall to a greater extent than
in the consumer field, and some of the smaller suppliers would
be forced into bankruptcy.

But in the industrial field the strike would be catastrophic.
Industrial salesmen could not be replaced by advertising or any
other form of sales promotion.

Why? Because more than in any other form of selling, the
industrial salesman is as much a consultant as a salesman.
Often, he has special qualifications in chemistry, engineering,
electronics, accountancy, or alternatively, he may have had
considerable product training. The industrial salesman, therefore, is able to help his buyers in many ways—in fact, they
often rely on him to solve problems for them and to keep them
up to date technically.

In industry, selling is the focal point in the dissemination of information, while in the consumer field, advertising plays the major role. Without a salesman's advice and guidance, many manufacturing projects would be held up. Consider the help given to buyers by salesmen of packaging, electronic devices, mining equipment, ventilation, safes, computers, fire detection equipment.

But back to our imaginary strike. Because those selling to industry have to impart information and advice to a greater degree than salesmen selling in any other field, their absence would cause a slowdown in production, and would affect the total economy of the country.

The highly improbable situation of a salesmen's strike has only been highlighted to emphasise *the importance to the community of the man who sells to industry.*

The Effect His Qualifications can Have on a Salesman

Knowledge of the importance of his work and pride in his qualifications have their dangers for the industrial salesman. He may believe that his value to buyers lies in his specialised knowledge rather than his ability as a salesman. He is still partly living in the Victorian era.

Then, we served the world, and the world begged for our ships, railways, woollen goods, chemical plants. Bewhiskered managing directors of those days had no need to send out salesmen to scour the continent for orders. Engineers travelled only to show blueprints; surveyors discussed projects. Why use selling techniques to emphasise product benefits when customers were flocking to buy? But buyers no longer queue for our products, and engineers have to *sell*. Technical knowledge by itself is not enough.

We are sometimes asked the question: Which is of greater importance for the industrial salesman, product knowledge plus technical qualification, or salesmanship?

The answer must be: *It all depends*—it all depends on whether a salesman is in a buyers' or a sellers' market. If the latter, then sales ability is not of such great importance—orders will be placed because of shortages; but when competition is really fierce even the industrial salesman who has won the friendship and regard of his buyers over many years of good service can find that he is sometimes left out in the cold. There is little loyalty when a competitor makes an offer which a buyer believes it will be to his advantage to accept.

The problem is to persuade a man with a logical mind, backed perhaps by a first-class degree, that an industrial salesman (there are many titles—sales engineer, technical representative, consultant—for the sake of simplicity, the title used in this book will, in the main, be industrial salesman) has to *sell* to succeed.

In fairness to the men who have worked so hard to achieve a degree or other qualifications, their attitude is understandable. They know that someone can be trained to become a good salesman in a matter of weeks or months while they, perhaps, have had to work hard for years to obtain their qualifications. But what if a competitor's salesmen have similar qualifications?

Here is a golden rule of selling: When all things are equal the orders usually go to the salesman with the greater *selling skills*.

Few of us can pass the *does it apply to me* test, but daily we should make the attempt. At least it could help us to be more tolerant. At the most, it can make us outstanding salesmen and far better members of the community. When we meet people who bore us by talking continuously about themselves, their children, their hobbies, how do we answer such questions as: *Am I like that? Do I ever bore people?* When the exaggerations and tall stories of others annoy us, do we ever consider whether we exaggerate or tell similar stories? Do we attempt to be funny men, closing in on others to tell them our tales? And that bright, colourful, flowery tie worn by the other fellow, if worn by us, becomes a floral masterpiece to tone with our trendy shirt.

Now read on, and honestly answer the question: *Does it apply to me?*

A common fault with many an industrial salesman is the dulling of a buyer's senses with sophisticated technical jargon. The years of training have given him his great understanding of chemistry, electronics, or engineering, which he believes must not be withheld. Every word must prove to the buyer the sales-man's complete grasp of the subject.

The snags are: most buyers don't like to feel inferior in knowledge to any salesman, although often they are; and, because some buyers are inferior in knowledge and may not know what the salesman is talking about, they are first bored, and then become annoyed.

Remember, a buyer has to have a reasonable all-round knowledge of the many products he buys, while the salesman is a specialist in one area.

Well, *does it apply to you?* Do you ever on occasion, stress the technicalities when you should be driving home customer benefits? The manner in which you analyse your own thoughts now is of major importance to you. Irrespective of the decisions you arrive at, what is important is the depth of the analysis.

Did you pause to play back in your mind some recent inter-views, to see whether you had talked technicality upon techni-cality? Or did you automatically discard the suggestion that, when selling, you could possibly be too technical?

Bear in mind, then, the great importance of your work—your importance to the community—and while appreciating and being proud of your technical knowledge, remind yourself that it is always the selling skills derived from this knowledge which are the formulae for success.

2

Salesmanship is Influencing Minds

To paraphrase Shakespeare, '*a salesman in his time plays many parts*' but for all that, the object of a salesman at every interview is to *persuade*.

The only exception is during times of acute shortages, when selling is unnecessary, and when the showing of a sample or a descriptive leaflet is sufficient to enable the buyer to place as large an order as the salesman is willing to accept. There are occasions when no selling is needed, even when there is a free flow of goods. For example, a company could hold a patent on a product or a component which competitors could not match in design or price.

When repeat business is a mere formality, company representatives could be called advisers, goodwill workers, stock checkers, or public relations officers—but they are not salesmen.

But if a buyer can say '*No*'—if a buyer can purchase similar equipment from a competitor—if a buyer can do without a product or service—if a buyer does not believe that he is in need of a product or service—then, however long the salesman has known the buyer, however friendly the relationship between them, the salesman has to use selling skills if he is to persuade the buyer to place an order.

Influencing Minds
There is an old selling cliché: *Selling only begins when the buyer says 'No'*.

That thinking has been proved completely wrong, but the cliché still persists.

As marketing begins with the germ of an idea in the research director's mind, so selling must always start at the pre-planning stage. Today's professional salesman, appreciating that it is much more difficult to turn a 'no' into a 'yes', plans his sales offer skilfully, so as to avoid that buyer's 'No'.

Few people will admit, 'You were right, I was wrong when I said "no".' But that is what the buyer must think when a salesman changes the 'no' to 'yes'. No buyer is happy at coming off second best, yet there are many occasions in selling when, in spite of pre-planning, a buyer has to be *persuaded* to change his mind; and when persuasion succeeds, a mind is influenced. If a buyer is antagonistic to a company or its products, the salesman, by persuasion, has to influence the mind of that buyer to overlook past mistakes. It is because it is so hard to influence a mind that selling, on occasion, can be difficult.

Here are five typical examples of problems faced regularly by industrial salesmen:

1. Mr. Johnson, of Johnson & Co., has used a power lift stacker manufactured by White & Co., for ten years. It has given satisfactory service, and should last another five years.

Smith, the salesman employed by White's competitors, Brown & Co., has to convince Mr Johnson that their new giant stacker will save money and time, have wider application, can meet almost any stacking requirement, and that the purchase should be made now, not in five years' time. If Mr Johnson is to buy, Smith has to change Mr Johnson's outlook completely on the problem of stacking goods efficiently.

2. Mr Green, of Green & Co., has for several years purchased a mechanical component for use in the manufacture of Green's products.

Harvey, the salesman employed by New Electronics Ltd, has to convince Mr Green that he should replace the known with the unknown—the mechanical component with an electronic component. Harvey has to influence Mr Green's mind so that Mr Green is prepared to take a risk with something new.

3. Mr Blue, of Blue & Co., has been buying anti-corrosion paint from Jones & Co., for fifteen years. (It must always be remembered that no product or service gives 100% satisfaction all the time. Ninety-nine per cent is the highest, and that is rarely achieved. There must always be at least a 5% doubt.)

Mr Longmay, salesman for Anti-Corrosion Paints Ltd, has to influence the mind of Mr Blue so that Mr Blue will no longer buy all his requirements from Jones & Co., in spite of the fact that he believes he has had satisfaction from them for fifteen years. The operative word is *believe*. Mr Longmay knows there must be a 5% doubt, and on this hinges his sales presentation.

4. A warehouseman is used to using ABC racking. A salesman from XYZ Racking has to convince the works director that his system will, in the long run, give more satisfactory results than that supplied by ABC and that, therefore, there should be a gradual changeover to his company's products. But the warehouseman sees no reason for a change.

Although he cannot buy, he can influence the thinking of his works director. The objective of the XYZ company salesman, therefore, is to change the mind of the warehouseman.

5. There are twenty draughtsmen in an office of a building contractor. Each has his likes and dislikes of the suppliers' products. Sometimes a salesman has to win over several of these men, if he is to finalise an order with the buyer.

In each of these cases a buyer's mind has to be influenced by the salesman.

Influencing the Buyer to Make the Right Decision

Selling in a competitive market when a buyer has to decide between conflicting claims is never easy, either for the buyer or the salesman.

Let us consider these examples:

Companies A, B, C and D, all supply a similar component part used in the manufacture of Unit Z.

Company A mass produce the component, which can easily be adapted for other uses. Their price is low and the component can be rated at 70% efficiency.

Company B manufacture a more expensive product than Company A, but it is durable, and is not often the cause of breakdown in the completed Unit Z. It rarely needs replacing. Rating 85%.

Company C are the market leaders, offering a well designed

and manufactured component with the added advantage of being able to offer quick delivery. Rating 80%.

Company D offer the most expensive component on the market, but they give superlative service, and have a back-up team of engineers on twenty-four hour call. Rating 90%.

When Salesman A calls he will attempt to persuade the buyer that the advantage of a lower price plus a good standardised product far outweigh any other consideration.

Salesman B might say, 'Mr Baker, the cost of replacements can be very high when you take into account loss of customer goodwill and the time taken up by your service engineers in replacing components still under guarantee. Of equal importance is the advantage your salesmen have. They can tell your customers that one of the most vital parts of your Unit Z is a component whose durability is guaranteed by the suppliers for two years.'

Salesman C might say, 'Mr Baker, one of the reasons why we are market leaders is because apart from the stringent testing of our range of components, as you know, the size of our organisation enables us to carry very large stocks. This means that when we say we can deliver in five weeks, in five weeks you will get the components. Think what this means to you in the way of a smooth production run!'

Salesman D might say, 'Mr Baker, you are right. We are more expensive than others, and there is a very good reason for this. We offer you the best value. Think what it means to you if Unit Z should stop working in Glasgow or Cardiff, or Worthing for that matter. Our engineer will call on your customer within twenty-four hours to check up on our component. And as you know, a back-up team is always available to help you with your technical problems related to the component and Unit Z.'

In each example, the salesman is trying to influence the mind of the buyer—always giving good reasons why the decision should go to him—and each salesman has a good case.

Salesman A will win sometimes, B, C, or D on other occasions, but each company's sales will largely depend on the ability of its salesmen. Results do not always depend on product claims, because every company honestly believes that it has the right policy and offers the best value. Results will nearly always depend on the aptitude of a salesman to apply that policy—his ability to *influence minds*.

A buyer has to decide between conflicting claims and a salesman has to highlight the particular claim or claims he can make for his product. The salesman's problem is the more difficult.

For him, there is only success or failure—an order, or a turn-down. The buyer will not fail completely, whatever his decision. Whichever reputable company he buys from, he will either buy well, or not so well, And however hard he tries, he won't be right every time. But because he does see, perhaps, five or six salesmen a day selling competing products, he can make life difficult for a salesman—difficult because it is rare for a salesman to be selling a product or service which is so far ahead of competition in every way (technically, price, delivery, after sales service) that a buyer will never give a second thought to a competitor's product.

Even if a salesman has such an overall advantage it will be shortlived. Nothing has ever been manufactured which cannot be copied within a reasonable time. Patents can hold competitors at bay for a while, but industrial groups have such vast resources that, if they cannot copy a patent or buy it, their research divisions will quickly come up with an alternative. Also, however well entrenched a salesman may be with a buyer —however sure he is that he will get nearly all of the business— the day will almost invariably come when the buyer will retire, leave for another position, or even be dismissed. Then, the salesman has to start all over again with a new buyer, who may have his own close friends in the selling world.

How, then, can a salesman succeed in face of a buyer's discrimination, of continual change, and of fierce competition? How can he learn to influence minds? The answer is for him not only to keep up to date on product knowledge, but so to increase his selling skills that his powers of persuasion are greater than those of his rivals.

Always Act in Your Company's Interest

A sales manager, referring to one of his salesmen said, 'He gives splendid service to his customers—I only wish he would give the same service to us.'

For too long the belief has been held that a salesman must act like a welfare officer, social worker, or probation officer—those people who selflessly give all their time to helping and advising others. Whether acting voluntarily or for reward, they invariably try to act in the best interests of the other person, irrespective of the cost in time to themselves.

But salesmen are not welfare officers. Their job is to sell. The industrial salesman only gives advice, guidance, and solves problems for one reason—the ultimate order. It is hypocritical to believe that a salesman is motivated by altruistic reasons to strive to solve customers' problems. He does so for a personal benefit—an eventual order; to retain goodwill; or to obtain repeat business.

But, of course, he gets a great deal of personal pleasure and gratification from the challenge of helping to solve problems for his customers. For all that, a salesman cannot be unbiased. Even when advising his customers, he must always act first in his company's interests. When a salesman puts his customers first and his company second he is acting in the interests of neither.

Here are examples showing how a salesman, perhaps unwittingly, can act against his company's interests:

Modification of Equipment

A buyer would have been quite willing to place an order for a standard industrial warm air unit. Like most buyers, however, he made comments, and one was a suggestion which he put forward mildly for a modification to the unit.

The salesman, instead of pointing out to the buyer that there was no need for such a modification, immediately agreed to contact his works director, and told the buyer that he was quite sure the modification could be carried out. The buyer, who did not feel strongly about the matter, emphasised that he was not prepared to pay any extra charge for the changes made.

For the manufacturer to have changed the specification and produced a one-only modified unit would have held up production lines, increased the cost, and involved extra work for an already over-stretched research and development division. To the annoyance of the salesman, the works director refused to make the modification without extra charge and the order was lost.

The salesman appealed to his sales director to change the decision, but his appeal made no impact, the sales director agreeing with his colleague on the board. The salesman felt that he had been badly let down, and wrote lengthy letters to his sales manager complaining that the refusal to help a valued customer would, undoubtedly, mean the loss of all this buyer's business.

The buyer who, in the first place, had been quite happy to buy a standard unit, then became annoyed at the refusal of the company to modify the unit without making an extra charge, and placed his order with a competitor.

Later, the salesman discovered that the competitor's warm air unit was almost identical with his own standard product, which he could so easily have sold in the first place.

Too many salesmen too readily want to satisfy their customers at their company's expense, when there is no need to do so.

A New Product Launch

A salesman received an inquiry. On following it up he learned from the buyer that the inquiry concerned the launching of a new product.

The buyer gave some details to the salesman of their needs if the project went ahead but explained that, as no final decision had been reached and his inquiry was still on the basis of research, the salesman should not involve himself too deeply. The buyer did not expect any of the suppliers to go to a great deal of trouble over the project until the board had given a further decision.

But the salesman did not repeat what the buyer had said to him when speaking to his sales manager, because he had already misled himself into believing that the project would go ahead, and that tremendous business would result. He stressed to his sales manager the huge potential, and the necessity of getting in on the ground floor.

His company's research and development division went to endless trouble, and put forward many ideas and drawings, the salesman persisting all the time that it would be worth while. Six months later the project was dropped.

The salesman's managing director telephoned the buyer and was told, 'We did explain to your Mr Smith (the salesman), when first we saw him, that you should not get too involved. Although we appreciate all you have done there was really no need for it. We only wanted to know whether we could co-operate, and if so, how long the design stage would take and when production could commence.'

The salesman's excuse was, 'I wanted to show them that we were the kind of company that would always go to endless trouble to help a customer.'

The rule for all industrial salesmen must be:

Give the customer the best possible service within the framework of your company's policy.

Most buyers are anxious to have the advice of industrial salesmen because these salesmen are specialists in their own fields— chemistry, electronics, computers, accounting machines, filing systems, ceramic insulators, plastic mouldings, machine tools, storage, or transport. But it cannot be repeated too often that the reason for giving advice is to achieve a final objective—a decision, and an order which will be profitable to the salesman's company.

This often means that the buyer has to re-think a project in terms of the supplier's interests as well as his own. This, in turn, means that if there is to be co-operation, the salesman has to influence the mind of the buyer to fall in with the design, production and delivery patterns of his company.

3

Selling by Objectives

One of the most dynamic influences on commercial and industrial growth occurred with the introduction of Management by Objectives.

MBO, as it became known, emphasised the need for each man within a working group to be given his own objective which, added to those of his colleagues, would lead to the achievement of the group objective.

The MBO concept is based on the fact that people work more effectively when they know precisely what they are trying to achieve. We have always known, at Tack, that this applies particularly to salesmen. For years every salesman in the Tack Group was given set targets—call targets, sales targets, targets for the number of appointments made by telephone, and for numbers of orders per quotation. Those attending our courses were given targets according to the specific requirements of their work.

When MBO emerged as a major factor in management techniques we realised that target setting was not precise enough. Targets or objectives should not relate only to the direct sales effort. They should be segmented. Each day a salesman should have a number of clearly defined objectives, ranging from having the best possible selling or demonstration kit, to the closing of an order.

With the advent of MBO we changed the title of Target Selling to Selling by Objectives.

Salesmen went from strength to strength as they appreciated the part each minor objective played in the reaching of the final objective—the order. Although the list of selling objectives is long (pre-planning itself is an objective), in the main, salesmen are concerned with call objectives.

Before every call a salesman must always have in his mind a

clear objective, otherwise he will lack purpose, arouse no interest and influence no one.

Here are examples of call objectives other than the closing of orders:

Visiting a Factory

John Wilson, a salesman for Lancing Ltd, decided that he would achieve a major step towards finalising an order if he could persuade Mr Brown, a works manager and a potential buyer, to visit the Lancing factory.

What, then, is the objective?

On the face of it, it is simply *to arrange a visit by Mr Brown to the factory.*

But is that the true objective? John Wilson is not offering Mr Brown a conducted tour of the factory, yet John might place the emphasis on the *visit* rather than on *the reason for the visit* when seeing Mr Brown, and that could cost him the order.

At the interview John might say something like this:

'You could see the Acme for yourself if you visited our factory, Mr Brown. Of course, I would pick you up in the car, take you to the airport, and accompany you to Manchester. One of our executives would meet the plane, you could have lunch with our directors, and this would give you the opportunity . . .'

Would that travelogue necessarily persuade Mr Brown to visit the factory? Perhaps, but possibly he might be concerned about the hospitality and feel that if he made the journey he might be committing himself to buy.

The emphasis, then, should not be on the *visit*, but on the *benefits* Mr Brown would derive from making that visit.

What is John's objective? First he must ask himself these questions:

Q. What is the reason for inviting Mr Brown to the factory?
A. Not to see the Acme in operation, but to see for himself the special features of the Acme—features which will be of direct interest and benefit to Mr Brown.

Q. Why should Mr Brown give up his time to make the long journey to Manchester?

A. Because at Brown's factory he has a labour problem, and the Acme can be operated by one man only. Also, Acme operators can be taught in three hours how to use the machine to the best advantage. Mr Brown would be able to satisfy himself on this point, because training schools are in progress all the time.

John Wilson now has a clear idea of his objective:

That Mr Brown should prove for himself the benefits offered by Acme units.

You will see how the emphasis has changed. No longer is John deeply concerned about travel arrangements or the hospitality at the factory. His objective is to persuade Brown that it is worth while putting himself out to see the Acme. *It is incidental that the Acme is at the Lancing factory. It could be anywhere.*

Wilson, knowing his true call objective, will be much more convincing in his arguments, and Mr Brown will be motivated to travel for the *right* reasons.

Dealing with a Complaint

One of your customers may be upset because he feels he has been let down (late delivery, wrong demand for settlement of an account, bad service). You have to call on him to straighten things out.

At first you might consider that the objective is to *deal with an objection*, but on reflection you may decide that a more correct objective would be to *restore confidence and to make sure of continuity of business*.

Your next task would be to set down minor objectives, which could be:

(a) To discover the true reason for the complaint and whether or not it is justified. Many complaints are wrapped up in side issues, generalisations, and reminders by buyers of what happened some years ago—all to confuse the issue.

On the company side, staff often try to justify their own mistakes.

(b) To find out how far you can go to put matters right. Is a company policy involved? Can extra credit be given? Can free service be given?

(c) To consider ways of ensuring that a similar complaint does not arise again.

(d) To rebuild the buyer's confidence in the company.

The final proof that all minor objectives and the call objective are achieved will be evinced when the buyer places further orders with you.

Here are some more typical call objectives:

> obtain payment of an overdue account, and retain good-will of customer
>
> when taking a quotation to a buyer, pinpoint special features which cannot be offered by competitors
>
> obtain information before seeking an interview with the buyer
>
> discover the true reason why an order is being held up
>
> survey premises prior to quoting

Selling by objectives enables a salesman to focus his mind on the real purpose of a call. Once that has been determined the interview with the buyer is not clouded by side issues, and this makes it easier for him to arrive at a favourable decision.

4

Identifying the Buyer

Why do salesmen attempt the impossible—selling to someone who cannot give a decision? It is always right to win over anyone who can influence an order, but that is different from giving a lengthy and complete sales offer to someone who only *imagines* he has sway with the buyer. There are two reasons for this ineffectual time wasting: One is inefficiency—slap-dash call preparation; the other, fear.

Many salesmen fear a confrontation with a buyer who holds a dominant position—managing director, financial director, works director. While they are quite happy seeing men of lesser status, they lack confidence when selling to top management. But this fear is quite irrational—there is no logical reason for a salesman to be afraid of any buyer. But life isn't always logical so, illogically, many men try to avoid being placed in a position where they can be overawed or given a direct refusal to buy. These salesmen, if questioned, excuse their psychological quirk with stock excuses:

'He can only be seen by appointment.'

'His secretary will never give appointments, except to her favourites.'

'It is essential to see Mr Brown first. He's the man who matters.' (He isn't!)

'Mr Smith has promised to pass on my information to the buyer, and I know he will be on my side.'

'It is a rule of the company that Mr White has to be seen first.'

'I've called a dozen times—you just can't see the buyer.'

'I honestly thought he could buy—he gave me the impression that he was the buyer.'

This self-delusion could be due to a feeling of inadequacy, a fear of being overwhelmed by a stronger personality, or a belief that the chief executive will conjure up unanswerable questions. But here is a fact. It is usually the assistant—junior buyer, a secretary, or local manager—who makes life difficult for salesmen. Nearly always, a top executive—be he managing director, works director, or financial director—is a very reasonable person to deal with.

A buyer may be protected by a host of people, but it is still a salesman's objective to skirt these guards and see the man who can decide.

Identifying the Influential

The salesman who knowingly wastes time with non-influential people is very different from the salesman who knows that a buyer appreciates the recommendations of his draughtsmen, assistant buyers product engineers, warehousemen, departmental managers, etc. A go-between, then, is either non-influential—seen only by a time-wasting salesman, or influential—may be seen regularly by a salesman. Both the buyer and those who can influence his decision must be identified. This is a primary objective. Fortunately, in most companies, there is a clearly defined buying chain.

> (The title *buyer*, used throughout this book means anyone who has the authority to buy, to make a final decision, or to authorise others to buy.)

There is no one better equipped to list buying procedures than Terry Pardoe, production director of Nu-aire (Contracts) Ltd (a division of the Tack Organisation). He has had a long and varied experience of industrial companies both large and small, and has lectured regularly on *Buying in Industry*. This is what he has to say on that subject:

'In the days of the very early cavemen a young man was being taught to hunt wild game by the elders of the tribe. He learned quickly and the day soon came when he faced his first sabre-toothed tiger.

'The tiger charged, and the young man took steady aim with his bow—but where should he aim? In the few seconds available, his logical mind provided an answer. He wanted the tiger to stop running; the tiger was running on legs; ergo, shoot for the legs!

'Unfortunately, because it was all so obvious to the tribal elders, nobody had thought to teach the young man about the basic anatomy of his target. What was obvious to them was not quite so obvious to him; he was forced to learn the hard way, with results that were less than satisfactory. But on the facts available to him at the time, it would have been very difficult to fault his reasoning.'

All right, so you don't believe the story.

Neither do you believe the one about the trainee salesman who returned to Head Office elatedly waving his first ever order for a new passenger lift—signed by the lift-attendant!

Maybe they are both silly stories, but what about this salesman's reasoning?

1. My job is to sell.
2. My prospective client employs a buyer.
3. The buyer's job is to buy.
4. I will therefore, obtain the best results by directing all my efforts at the buyer.

On the face of it the logic is irrefutable, but the salesman has ignored or had no knowledge of the anatomy of the company, and therefore incorrectly directed his aim at what seemed to him to be the most obvious place.

But *obvious*, and *effective*, are not synonymous.

For the salesman selling to a manufacturing concern, a working knowledge of its anatomy is just as important to his prosperity as a knowledge of the tiger's anatomy was to our caveman's life.

The object of this chapter, then, will be to examine some of the *vital organs* of a manufacturing company—to see how they interact and depend upon one another. Armed with a basic understanding of how the organisation works, a salesman will be much better prepared to recognise when and where his efforts should really be directed for maximum effect.

The Vital Organs of the Manufacturer

The organisation of each manufacturing concern differs in some way from every other. But every manufacturer makes his profit by buying goods and materials, changing them in some way, then selling the resultant product. To do this there are a number of basic operations which must be performed, irrespective of the size of the organisation or the nature of the end product.

At one end of the spectrum, that of the one-man firm, the proprietor may perform all these operations himself. At the other, each of the basic operations will be the concern of a separate highly specialised department. The primary basic operations may even be further subdivided in an effort to increase efficiency by yet greater specialisation.

Let us consider then, some of the primary, or essential, basic functions of a medium-sized organisation.

Sales

An important part of the marketing function is to identify market needs and opportunities, and to pass this information on to the board of directors. If the proposal appears to have any merit, it will begin a long and complex process before full-scale design and production work can be authorised. This process usually involves a market survey, a design feasibility study, an evaluation of available manufacturing resources and a financial study.

Assuming that all these hurdles are successfully overcome, a new project becomes the responsibility of the design department.

The Design Department

This department has many an alias—development, research, laboratory, engineering, drawing office. Their prime task is to design a product which will meet a specified market requirement.

The starting point is a *sales specification*, and the theoretical finishing point is a prototype model, design drawings and a performance specification.

During the design process the designers will call upon not only their own skills and knowledge, but also upon those of their colleagues in other departments. Often, they will seek also specialist assistance from existing or potential component or material suppliers.

Production Engineering Department (P.E.D.)

Production engineering is a ubiquitous department. Very broadly, it can be said that its function is to specify *how* the product should be made, and to provide the manufacturing departments with the equipment needed to make it.

Within this rather sweeping generalisation are hidden many detailed tasks and responsibilities. In practice, the department ends up by providing comprehensive technical support on just about every imaginable aspect of the product, plant, production process, and even, in many cases, the factory building itself.

Looked at in the narrower context of a new product, on which they will almost certainly have been consulted at the design stage, the production engineers must turn that new product into a practical manufacturing proposition.

This will require them to break the product down into its individual components and to examine each in detail, specifying exactly how they are to be manufactured. To meet the requirements of the performance specification in the most economic manner they will look at the questions of in-house manufacture versus outside purchasing; utilisation of existing plant and tools versus new acquisitions; use of machine A versus machine B; the need for new shop layouts, and so on.

Once these main decisions have been made P.E.D. will prepare detailed manufacturing instructions for each component, as well as for final assembly, and possibly inspection and test.

Throughout, they will have been working to a budget for plant and tooling, as well as for the finished product, and P.E.D. or a separate estimating department, will prepare detailed estimates of manufacturing costs for control purposes.

Associated with production engineering is often a work study function, whose responsibility it is to ensure that process costs remain within, or improve upon the estimated costs. The sales-man with a cost-saving proposition might well find some very powerful allies in this area.

Production Control Department (P.C.D.)

Responsible for the logistics of manufacturing operation, pro-duction control must translate customers' orders into a manu-facturing programme. They then ensure that men, materials, and machines are all brought together at the right time to meet their planned programme.

This they do by first informing the production shops of their forward load, usually in the form of men and machine hours derived by multiplying estimated or work-studied times by the number of items to be made. P.C.D. then ensures that the materials are made available when needed. The provision of materials is usually the direct responsibility of production con-trol, but is delegated in some concerns to a separate department, material control. The head of this department may or may not be subordinate to the production control manager, depending upon the particular set-up.

Usually, supplies of the majority of raw materials and com-ponents must be secured well in advance of receiving firm orders for the finished product. Maintaining stock levels that provide the optimum balance between on the one hand in-sufficient stock, which can create long delivery times, and on the other, excessive stocks which gobble up capital, is a very delicate business.

There are numerous approaches to the problem, but all involve either an analysis of past materials usage, or a forecast of future sales. Well, almost all! A colleague of mine recently asked the president of an important American manufacturer what forecasting system they used. 'Well Brian,' came the dis-armingly honest reply, 'we don't forecast—we just run out!' I suspect, in practice, that they are no worse than most of us, who forecast—and still manage to run out.

However, most systems involve an *explosion* of the parts list. This simply means that the list of parts and materials needed to make the product is multiplied by the quantity of the product expected to be made in a given period. By applying a series of standard mathematical formulae to the result—or by sheer guess work—or, as in every organisation of which I have had experience, by an inspired mixture of both, certain standard parameters are set for each item.

As the method of calculation varies from system to system, so does the terminology; but the two main parameters are the level to which stock will be allowed to fall before a repeat order is placed (usually called the re-order point) and the quantity to be re-ordered (re-order quantity).

Most material control systems are arranged so that re-ordering action is automatically triggered by the re-order point being reached. The replenishment orders may be internal; upon a machine shop or press shop for instance; or external, for bought-out components and materials. Usually, material control will give purchasing authority to buy, probably in the form of a purchase requisition, specifying the quantity and delivery date required. Purchasing will then be left to handle the actual mechanics of selecting the supplier, agreeing prices, placing the order, and subsequently progressing deliveries. The value of the order will generally decide how it is dealt with: by the chief buyer, or by a junior assistant, for bulk delivery, against a staggered delivery schedule, or even, sometimes, on a *call-off* basis against a *blanket order*.

Purchasing Department

Sometimes independent, sometimes subordinate to production control, the purchasing department has been described as production's solicitor. Buying little on its own behalf, purchasing seeks suppliers, vets them, negotiates contracts with them, assists them, kicks them occasionally, and sometimes replaces them; but always on behalf of some other department to which purchasing is providing a service.

A manufacturer resorts to purchasing from an outside supplier for one or more of a number of reasons, chief amongst which are:

(a) The manufacturer does not have the specialised technical knowledge available to allow the item or material to be designed and produced economically within his own organisation.

(b) Capital expenditure on the necessary plant and floor space is not justified.

(c) The labour capacity is not available.

This applies not only to components and materials, but also to items of capital equipment.

In some areas the make/buy decision is self-evident, and decided by broad company policy. The number of shirt manufacturers, for instance, who design and build their own sewing machines must be very limited indeed.

In other areas the decision is somewhat less clear cut. Is an extra press justified in the sheet metal working shop to make a new component? Should the work be sub-contracted until yet more work becomes available for the press?

Quite obviously, in neither case does the make/buy decision rest with purchasing, although they will play a large part in helping production management and the board to reach a decision. Nevertheless, at this stage, their role will be limited to advice on the availability and reliability of outside capacity, and the cost of buying out.

Purchasing will play a much more prominent part in a later stage of the process—the actual selection of the successful supplier. But in many, many cases, the selection of the supplier has already been so strongly influenced by another department that the purchasing department's eventual selection is almost a formality. This usually happens when design or production engineering have been exposed to technical assistance or advice from a supplier at an early stage of development and the supplier has been able to guide the design or manufacturing process towards the use of his product. The potential supplier willing to invest serious effort at this stage, whilst not necessarily home and dry, is most certainly half-way down the course before his rivals have even started. However, we are still left with a great many items which are bought against specifications, standard or otherwise. Nuts, bolts, steel bar and sheet, are examples which spring to mind. Although samples may sometimes be submitted to technical departments for checking, the purchasing department is seldom influenced by other departments when buying in this area. Production control or material control will decide the quantities and delivery dates needed, but thereafter, purchasing are on their own. Their selection will be based on considerations of price, delivery, and past experience of the quality of the supplier's product and service.

The suppliers of special items, once selected, are unlikely to be replaced unless a competitor can offer a very distinct advantage, but the supplier of standard items may well find himself on a short-list of *equal or approved* suppliers. Each time a repeat order falls due, purchasing will quickly check which supplier is currently offering the best deal (this can be based on quality, price, delivery, etc.), and that is where the order will be placed.

The purchasing department is not, therefore, necessarily the right place for a salesman to direct his main efforts. The successful salesman may negotiate and obtain the actual order from them eventually, but usually his real selling efforts will have been directed elsewhere, long before he gets to the final stage.

Vetting suppliers is an important facet of the work of purchasing departments. Usually, vetting takes the form of a visit to a manufacturing plant by a technical representative of the potential client. It may be someone from production engineering, quality control, or even production control. The object is to find out if production capacity, technical ability, and quality assurance arrangements appear adequate to meet their needs.

If you get to the point where you are being vetted, you are well in the running for a substantial order. Always seize this chance to show a customer what an asset you would be to him as a supplier.

These, then, are the key areas at which the selling effort should be directed. They are not, by any means, the only areas in which success can be achieved, simply the areas likely to prove most fruitful to the majority of salesmen.

You must analyse where the interest in your product is likely to lie, who stands to benefit from it, and who is able to influence (not necessarily to *authorise*) a decision to buy.

If you are selling electronic test equipment—convince the quality manager first. Industrial medical supplies—the factory nurse. A degreasing product for oil-impregnated floors, the maintenance engineer.

Although these may be the key areas for the salesman, for the manufacturer they are only part of his overall organisation.

The diagram on page 36 shows a typical organisational structure of a medium-sized manufacturing concern. You may never meet one exactly like it—some will have functions integrated; others will have them further sub-divided. The chain of command will vary from one company to another. A particularly common variation is found in the small to medium-sized company, where the managing director is the general manager, and the other members of the board are all working executives discharging the routine duties of sales manager, works manager, etc.

Study this diagram. Once you can remember who to expect to be responsible for what, you will not have too much difficulty when in a plant in finding variations on the basic theme by asking questions. Properly approached, I have never known anyone to take offence at such questions; in fact, most people enjoy the opportunity to show off their knowledge.

A Case Study
Northern Screwdrivers Ltd, had for many years been manufacturing small hand tools including insulated screwdrivers—the type that have a chrome-plated steel blade moulded into a simple plastic handle.

The salesmen had often been asked by wholesalers whether they manufactured an electrician's test-screwdriver. This device is a small screwdriver with a miniature neon lamp and resistor enclosed in a hollow handle, electrically connected between the

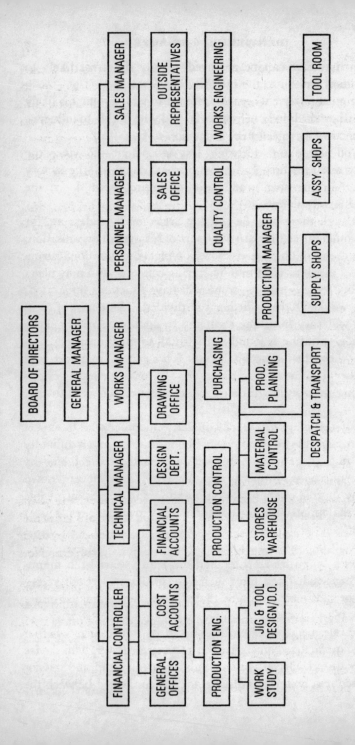

TYPICAL STRUCTURE OF A MANUFACTURING ORGANISATION

screwdriver blade and a metal pocket clip, similar to those used on fountain pens. The electrician holds the screwdriver by its insulated handle, making sure that he is touching the metal clip. He brings the blade of the screwdriver into contact with an electrical terminal and the neon lamp glows if the terminal is live. The electrician thus has a very cheap, convenient, and simple test instrument combined with a screwdriver, for little more than the cost of a conventional screwdriver.

The requests filtered through to the sales director who, after checking with a number of wholesalers, decided there was a viable market available if the price was right.

The proposition was put to the Board, who asked for a forecast of probable sales volumes at various selling prices. Once this was obtained the problem was passed to the design department, charged with producing a design and cost appraisal.

Design looked at the problem, and eventually produced drawings and a hand-made prototype. This, when broken down, consisted of seven separate components:

1. The blade
2. The moulded handle
3. The pocket clip
4. A moulded screw top to retain the pocket clip
5. A neon lamp
6. A resistor
7. A helical contact spring

The company had been making screwdrivers for many years, and were already geared up for the manufacture of blades and handles. The moulded screw top could be produced by their existing moulding machines, so that was no problem. New mould tools would be needed, but no plant.

Production Engineering were asked to estimate production and tooling costs for these items, and this they were able to do readily, and with accuracy. The buy/make decision made itself.

The buy/make decisions for the neon lamp and resistor also made themselves—but where to buy from did not.

At this very early stage, Design consulted one of the proprietary purchasing directories, and sent off a standard letter to each of the firms listed as electronic component suppliers. The letter gave a description of what was required, an estimate of the annual quantity envisaged, and asked simply for a quotation on this basis.

Some companies sent a quotation, some did not. But one sent a salesman, who brought along a newly developed lamp which not only had a contact at each end, ideal for this particular application, but had the resistor moulded in to form an integral part of the main component.

Although a little more expensive than the competition, it did have certain advantages which would allow the use of a simpler and cheaper handle moulding.

Purchasing were asked to make a preliminary discreet check on the supplier's standing, because they were not a nationally known name. An inquiry from a junior buyer of an ex-colleague, now working for a manufacturer of electronic equipment, produced the information that they were only a small company but they were working hard for their orders, and seemed to be reliable.

This was sufficient at this point to allow the preliminary design work to go ahead incorporating this particular neon.

Design found a suitable contact spring, sketched it, and asked Purchasing to obtain quotations. This, again, took the form of a standard letter to the listed spring manufacturing specialists. The resulting quotations were passed back to Design, who made their choice and used it in their provisional costings.

Production Engineering were consulted on the question of making or buying the spring clip. Its manufacture was a press-work job, but no suitable press was available within the factory. Some presswork was already being sub-contracted, but it was now beginning to look as if there might be a case for buying their own press.

Purchasing were asked for the bought-out quantities and prices of existing pressed components. At the same time they obtained a quotation from two or three presswork sub-contractors for the new spring clip. A glance through the trade journals produced a budget price for a new press of the capacity needed.

Cost Accounts and Estimating now got together informally to produce a comparison of the likely cost of continuing to buy from outside for the next five years, against the cost of internal manufacture, including amortised capital and maintenance costs. The recommendation was to buy a new press, so the matter was referred to the works manager who, knowing the Board's attitude, told Production Engineering to go ahead with their costings on the basis that a new press could be bought.

Design and Production Engineering were now in a position to submit firm estimates of costs and capital expenditure, as well as their prototype, to the Board.

The sales director had, meanwhile, been looking more closely at the new screwdriver's sales potential, so the Board had all the information needed to make the decision to go ahead or abandon the project. They decided to go ahead.

Further drawings were prepared and amended. Prototypes were made and tested. Drawings were further amended and checked again.

Purchasing arranged for formal vetting of the neon lamp manufacturer, but because of the vital nature of this component the vetting was in far greater depth than usual. A visit was made by the works manager, the production engineering manager, and the quality manager to their factory. The financial director obtained copies of their past accounts from Companies House, and information on their credit worthiness from an insurer specialising in the insurance of commercial debts.

Neon Lamps Ltd passed the tests. Small, but sound, they knew their business.

Meanwhile, tooling quotations had been obtained for the plastic mould tools. Long and hard experience had led them to become ultra-conservative in this area! Because this was capital expenditure, the quotations went to the Board for approval; but as they were within the overall budget already approved in principle by the Board, approval for the tooling was a mere formality.

The final decisions involved the press and associated tooling.

Production Engineering asked technical representatives from several well-known machine-tool manufacturers to visit them. Each company sent a representative, who discussed the requirements with a senior production engineer.

Out of the discussions emerged three possible presses, all of the same order of cost. There was very little to choose between them, but the salesman from Squashing Presses Ltd, had put the production engineer in touch with a toolmaker specialising in press tools—an area where the production engineer had only limited experience. When this toolmaker was contacted he proved not only highly competent, but helpful as well.

The three alternatives had to go to the works manager for the final choice to be made, then the firm proposal to spend capital on a particular machine had to receive formal Board approval.

When the purchase requisition went through to Purchasing, it was not for *a* 50 ton press, but for *the* Model B 50 ton press made by Squashing Presses Ltd.

This, then, was how the first and most vital buying decisions were made.

It is worth looking back to summarise these items, and the areas where the real selling took place.

ITEM	INITIAL EFFORT	CONFIRMING EFFORT
Neon lamp/resistor	Design	The vetting team
Contact Spring	Purchasing	Quality Control
Mould Tools	Production Engineering	Quality Control and Production Management
Press	Production Engineering	Works Manager
Press Tools	The Press Manufacturer	Production Engineering

It has been said that when a manufacturer buys, he does so to solve a problem. The salesman who demonstrates that his product is the answer to that problem, and who can guide the customer away from a serious consideration of the alternative solutions, must create a tremendous advantage for himself. To do so he must see all of those people who can influence the decision and make his main effort at the *right place at the right time*.

Remember always that the manufacturer has chosen to make his living by buying goods, modifying them, and selling the resultant product at a profit.

If he omits the modifying stage he is a merchant. If he omits the buying and selling stages he is out of business!

In the process of making his profit the supplier's salesman is a vital link.

Only if the supplier's propositions are *effectively aimed and timed* can both parties gain the full benefit of this relationship.

5

Buyer Analysis

The potter moulds clay and the sculptor fashions marble, but the salesman changes people, calming the irascible, getting the attention of the unattentive, and turning a buyer's *no* into *yes*. Each day, salesmen motivate people, and the importance for a salesman to prepare for every human contingency cannot be over-emphasised. Salesmen do not have to be psychologists to appreciate that Jung's theory applies especially to buyers.

Jung divided people into three psychological categories:
  thinking
  feeling
  intuitive

Let us forget people generally, and consider the application of Jung's theory to buyers.

The 'Thinking' Buyer

He is logical in his thinking and will immediately condemn a salesman who exaggerates, who cannot substantiate a claim, or who talks on and on without making a definite point.

Here is an example of a 'thinking' buyer:

One of our sales staff employed by Personnel Hygiene Services Ltd, called on the buyer of one of the largest hotel chains. Her purpose was to explain why prices had to be increased. (P.H.S. provides a monthly hygiene service carried out by service girls.)

The buyer said, 'Your competitor called yesterday and quoted the same service figure as previously. In view of salary increases and inflation I knew this was not possible, unless their service suffered. I don't like paying extra, but I like bad service even less.'

We got the order.

The 'Feeling' Buyer

This person, while still requiring facts, will also respond emotionally to a salesman's appeal. He is not so cold and calculating as the 'thinking' buyer.

An example of the 'feeling' type of buyer was provided by a delegate at one of our sales training courses. He said, 'I was explaining the benefits and virtues of a chemical for use in a manufacturing process, but making little headway. Then I told him that the chemical polluted neither air nor water. This immediately aroused the buyer's interest. Apparently he is a very keen fisherman, and hates to think of the fish being destroyed by polluted water. His whole manner changed from then on.'

The 'Intuitive' Buyer

This buyer believes that he has an extra sense—some insight which allows him to arrive at correct decisions more often than others not gifted with his type of intuitive mind.

It is not always easy for a salesman to recognise which type of buyer he is dealing with at a first call, but after several calls he will be able to type the *thinking, feeling* or *intuitive* buyer, and vary his sales techniques accordingly.

Although the features of a product do not vary, the words used for describing these features should change, according to the buyer's mentality and the kind of appeal most acceptable to him.

Managing Directors

Having segregated buyers into their psychological categories, next one must consider their idiosyncrasies, the reasons for their actions, and the parts they play on the stage of the industrial theatre.

If you are selling capital goods, managing directors are nearly always directly involved, and in the medium sized or smaller companies they are usually closely concerned with every aspect of buying. Some managing directors—especially the entrepreneural types—when buying in association with others (directors, managers, committees) highlight their own importance in several ways:

1. *The self-effacing.* This type of managing director conveys the impression that he is listening carefully to the views of his colleagues but, in point of fact, his mind may well be made up very early in the salesman's presentation. His thoughts are: *Let the others talk—I'll come in at the proper time to make the most impact.* Indirectly, therefore, the salesman must be selling to that managing director.

2. *The self-denigrating.* He will often say, 'I delegate, and forget. This isn't really my concern you know.' When, of course, everyone knows that it *is* his concern and that he is the decision maker. The salesman takes a risk when he believes this man and concentrates on the subordinates.

3. *The strong man.* This type is brusque to the point of rudeness. His sentiments are: *I'll show everyone round here who's boss!* This is usually an act, and need not frighten the salesman.

4. *The kindly and friendly.* The managing director knows his own importance, and can be very friendly. No salesman should attempt to take advantage of his attitude and become familiar.

5. *The short and sharp.* He will say, 'Remember, I'm a very busy man, as are my associates—so don't waste our time.' He will listen for hours if the salesman has marshalled his facts and presents them correctly, but will cut him short if the presentation becomes repetitive.

6. *The sharpshooter.* This managing director constantly interrupts the salesman when he is in full flight. The managing director has a very quick mind and is usually ahead of the salesman in his thinking.

When selling to the sharpshooter the salesman should curtail his sales presentation, keep to facts only, and never, never exaggerate.

These men's attitudes should not be misunderstood. They are usually able, sometimes brilliant, and generally very likeable people, but they have to emphasise their own importance. This is a fundamental of human relations applicable

to many people—as much to Prime Ministers as to works fore-
men, to sales directors and to their salesmen. A managing director might control twenty thousand people and a turnover of
many millions, but he can still be unsure that everyone realises
how important he is. Why else do men of this calibre drop
names, refer to calls made upon their time by Government
departments, yearn for decorations or titles? Others show
photographs of their dogs (making sure that the country house
is well pictured in the background).

Before trade union officials say, 'Typical of top brass!' they
should realise that they are not exempt from the need to feel
important. They, too, put over the same act as the rest of us.
Although, so far, we are considering selling to managing directors, it is worth while emphasising that a prime lesson for all
salesmen is that almost everyone likes to build his own importance.

The salesman who is genuinely interested in the work of a
machine operator, for example, and who shows his concern for
that machinist's skill and the importance of the job he is doing,
will make that man feel better. And when the buying decision
is reached, the advice of that man may well be sought. The
salesman who seeks the advice of a production manager's
secretary is building her importance.

While the amateur salesman always builds up his own standing in an attempt to outrival the knowledge of a buyer, the
professional salesman will always show strength by making it
clear that he realises the importance of the other man's position.
He is right, because every man involved in a buying decision
has a vital task to fulfil, and this should be acknowledged by the
salesman. Many, many orders have been lost through lack of
understanding of this simple aspect of human behaviour, which
seems to be inherent not only in managing directors, but in all
of us—the need to feel important.

Finally, remember that the vast majority of managing directors are not ruthless men. They will always try for a better
bargain, but if you have offered the best terms, if your product is
competitive, and if you stand firm by your rights, you will win

many more times than you lose. Managing directors do respect the ability of others, which means they respect the professional salesman.

The Unmentionable Buyer

Over the years there has been, on occasion, wide press coverage of events leading up to the trial of someone accused of accepting bribes for giving preferential treatment to a supplier, builder, architect, or local Government official. There is such publicity because bribery in industry is so rare. There will always be an occasional black sheep buyer, as there are black sheep doctors, solicitors, policemen—but there are very, very few tainted men in the professions or in Government employ, and the same applies to industry.

The reason why it seems to be rampant is because salesmen *and* sales managers have to find excuses for failure.

When a salesman loses an order he feels certain he should have had he will say, '*Everyone knows* that X (the buyer) is on the make.'

The key word is *everyone*. Whenever anyone wants his (or her) statement to be accepted as true he will begin:

'*Everyone knows* . . .' or

'*Everyone says* . . .' or

'*This is on very good authority* . . .'

But these words are only a camouflage for rumour. No one can ever pinpoint the *everyone*.

If you fail to get an order, try to find out the *real* reason. You can be assured that whatever rumours abound, it will *very* rarely, if ever, be due to bribery.

Entertaining

Another subject which must be included in buyer analysis is entertaining. We hear stories of buyers having wild nights with call girls, being fêted on yachts, or holidaying in Mediterranean chateaux owned by company managing directors.

Again, these facts are rarely substantiated. For the industrial salesman, entertaining *can* cement a friendship, and it does allow a buyer to talk over his problems and conduct negotiations away from a busy factory or office, where there may be constant interruptions. Entertaining at this level is not unethical. No buyer is going to place an order just because a salesman has bought him a dinner. Only if the quality of a product is right, competitive in price, service, etc., and is what the buyer needs, does friendship play a part in selling. When it doesn't matter to the buyer whether he places an order with company A, B or C, it is nearly always the able salesman with the closest relationship with the buyer who will get the order. Entertaining can help to cement that relationship.

But entertaining must be kept in perspective. It might be right for a managing director to take another managing director or chief executive to Claridge's or the Dorchester. It is rarely necessary for a salesman to entertain at this level.

I should now like to destroy the myth that all chief executives eat like gourmets and drink only the finest wines.

I suppose I have been dined out by, or have dined, as many chairmen and managing directors of companies as anyone. I can count on the fingers of one hand the number who ate other than sparingly, and the majority drank very little if at all.

A buyer knows that the meal is on the expense account, so it is of little use to act the part of a millionaire to try to impress him. Many industrial buyers, and men who can influence orders, prefer lunch at the local pub to a dinner at an expensive restaurant. Buyers do like a salesman who acts naturally, and they do not like to see money thrown away.

There are, of course, the exceptions, but these exceptions who want 'top hat' treatment are rarely influenced by a salesman who is generally no closer to the order at the end of the meal than at the beginning. Never believe the promises of this type of buyer. He forms no real friendships, in spite of considerable entertaining. He has been taken out so often, and he cannot buy from everyone. You lose nothing with this man by not taking him out at all.

To sum up the position: except for the tiny minority who

look forward to being fêted, the majority of buyers, ranging from young highly skilled university trained technicians to middle-aged production chiefs, development engineers, or project engineers, while enjoying being entertained do not look for lavishness. These conclusions were substantiated by a Tack Survey. *Entertain sensibly—it can cement a friendship.*

The Talkative Buyer

This buyer's defence mechanism is his ability to out-talk the most verbose saiesman. The sales offer quickly gets bogged down, and if the buyer has his way, never emerges. Not only does he continually elaborate a train of thought, but interrupts a salesman to tell a long involved story with only a slight bearing on the salesman's argument.

The talkative buyer will sidetrack the salesman in many ways. He will speak about left wing or right wing politicians, trade unions, or the difficulties of management, of sport, or staff, or his hobbies ... He will also like to reminisce—'I remember once when I was offered ... of course you know Brown & Co., well I remember when they first made ...'

After some ten minutes of chat this buyer will often say, 'Thanks for calling. I'm afraid I'm rather busy this morning. Can you leave me that (brochure, leaflet, photograph, drawing) and I'll be in touch.'

The interruption technique is the best way of selling to the talkative buyer. The salesman should interrupt when he can do so without being discourteous. For example:

> 'That is a most interesting point you've made, Mr Smith, there's too much form filling in business today, that is why ...'

or,

> 'Mr Smith, forgive me for interrupting you, but what you have just said is vital to industry, because ...'

This technique is usually acceptable, but it can falter if the salesman is half-hearted in his interruption. He must speak strongly, and then immediately revert to his sales offer.

Once the talkative buyer listens to a salesman without

constantly interrupting, he can be involved in the real purpose
of the call.

The Too-Friendly Buyer

A buyer may be abrupt, curt, almost rude, but he may also
listen carefully to a salesman's proposition. The brusque buyer
is not too difficult a man to overcome, but the over-friendly
buyer can make life very hard for the salesman.

He seems to agree with everything, but still doesn't buy. This
buyer greets a salesman pleasantly, but this is a disguise. He
knows that while he is being so friendly it is hard for the salesman to *sell*. The timid salesman is always impressed with
friendliness, and will write on his report to head office:

> 'Mr Brown greeted me in a most friendly way. He listened
> to everything I had to say, and agreed with our proposition.
> He would not come to an immediate decision but he is,
> undoubtedly, a very good prospect. I feel sure that next
> time I call I shall get an order."

But he won't get an order. The buyer will be just as friendly
on the next occasion, saying, 'I told you last time that I like
your product, but I'm not quite ready for it.'

To tackle a friendly buyer needs strong will power. If the
buyer agrees, the strong salesman will immediately ask for the
order. The more friendly the buyer becomes, the more strongly
(but in the gentlest but firmest way) the salesman should sell.
He knows the buyer for what he is worth, and will not be shown
to the door with the buyer's arm around his shoulders and a
'thank you for calling'. The only thanks he wants for calling is
the signed order. A buyer's friendship is proved when he gives
you orders.

The Buyer Who is Scared of Buying

With a scared or timid buyer, confidence building must have a
high priority in the sales offer. This buyer won't buy unless
he has complete confidence in a supplying company. For
this reason it is wrong to ask the timid buyer for his advice,
something that most buyers appreciate. He will consider it

a sign of weakness, and will conclude that the salesman is not competent.

With this buyer there must be no equivocation. No alternative should be offered. The salesman should determine exactly what he wants the buyer to buy, and then keep to that decision.

This buyer is so afraid of making a mistake, although probably the real mistake was in placing him in the position of having to make buying decisions. There are many first class project engineers, works managers, office managers, quite capable of running their section efficiently, but still afraid of making buying mistakes.

The salesman selling to this buyer must remember that there is nothing so contagious as enthusiasm—*except the lack of it*.

Once confidence has been established the enthusiasm of a salesman can inspire the scared buyer to overcome his fears and become equally enthusiastic about a product or service. But a word of warning. This buyer is difficult to recognise at a first call. He may even look tough and determined, but his rough exterior hides a quaking stomach. His standard ploy to get rid of a salesman is: 'I'll have to put this before . . .' Of course he could make the decision himself, but he can't rid himself of his fear of a mistake. Once the salesman has built up trust in himself and his company, however, he will find that the scared buyer can become a very loyal customer.

The Taciturn Buyer

This man is the opposite of the compulsive talker. He says little, often signalling acquiescence by a grunt rather than by saying 'Yes' which, he feels, might commit him. The taciturn person is usually introspective, and almost the perfect listener, except that his listening doesn't seem to bring him any nearer to arriving at a decision.

Adroit questioning will force the taciturn buyer to become involved in the sale, provided that the questions are directly pertinent to the buyer's business. The salesman will find that by this method, this type of buyer will sometimes even answer

at length, and the salesman will know then that he is involving
the buyer in the sales offer.

The Bluffer

These memos to a sales manager at head office are the results
of a salesman calling on the *bluffer:*

Memo No. 1.

> I was with Mr Evans today. He wants us to quote for 150
> Sponlites Mark II. He didn't seem at all worried about the
> cost—he knows the total order with spares will be in excess
> of £30,000.

Memo 2.

> Mr Evans is very interested in the quotation—thank you
> for getting it through so quickly. He now wants an amended
> quote for 110 Sponlites Mark II and 80 Sponlites Mark
> III. Naturally, I am delighted as this will substantially
> increase the order. It will be the largest I have ever taken,
> and I know he is not even going to Hardwicks' for a quote.

Memo 3.

> I took the revised quote to Mr Evans but he was too busy
> to see me. However, he left a message to say he would
> telephone.

Memo 4.

> I saw Mr Evans today. He is very impressed with the quote,
> the layout, and the drawings, which he thought excellent.
> I have to call next week.

Memo 5.

> Mr Evans told me that as the order is now in excess of
> £40,000 it has to be finally sanctioned by the Board, but he
> says that will cause no problem.

Memo 6.

> Mr Evans is away on holiday.

Memo 7.

> Bad news I'm afraid. The Board have refused to sanction
> the order because of the credit squeeze, but Mr Evans
> assures me that I have nothing to worry about. The order
> will be ours as soon as the squeeze is lifted.

Memo 8.

> I am sorry to have to tell you that Mr Evans has installed 6 Donolites (Hardwicks' products). This really shook me, until he said that I was not to worry, the big order will be ours when . . .

The never-ending saga of the salesman who believed the Bluffer—the person who thinks big, but buys small.

The Bluffer misleads a salesman in another way when he says, 'I never play about. It's either the lot or nothing, for me! We shall replace all the elecophones or none at all, and I want to do the whole job.'

The salesman feels he is winning and the buyer continues, 'But this all ties up with other top management plans. So come back and see me in about six months' time, and then I shall be ready to talk business.'

The salesman goes away starry-eyed, convinced that he will get a big order in six months' time.

The way to tackle this buyer is to try to give him what he really wants, without cutting him down to size.

The salesman might say to the buyer interested in elecophones.

> 'Mr Brown, I appreciate that you will want to install about two hundred elecophones to cover the whole building, but I would like to suggest that you do the corner block first. Some of our biggest accounts started with us by testing our claims for themselves and subsequently they all switched over completely. Now that will only mean an initial outlay of . . .'

How do you recognise the Bluffer? First, if he has played the game with you before; second, he sometimes gives himself away by his apparent eagerness to buy big. While the man who buys big goes very closely into every aspect of a proposition, the Bluffer doesn't ask any questions, nor does he question again the salesman's claims

BUT

if there is the slightest doubt in your mind, if you are not at least 90% sure you are being bluffed, then you must go out for the big order.

If you have been bluffed once you will know better, next time.

The Stubborn Buyer

When the stubborn buyer has made up his mind, nothing seems to budge him. Any hint of criticism will lose the order. He would rather make a wrong decision than change his mind.

His problem is psychological—he is afraid of appearing weak. He is the kind of man who will tell you that he always believes in admitting it when he is in the wrong; unfortunately, he always believes he is right. The strength of your sales presentation enables you to sell to him. If he has raised an objection, he doesn't like to be proved wrong.

A presentation which forestalls objections lets him feel that he is making all the decisions, all the time.

The Busy Buyer

You know how it is in offices when the boss walks in. Everyone, even the typists who have nothing to do except polish their nails, acts as if the work is really piling up for him. Do they mislead the boss? Not at all! But both sides enjoy the act.

It's no different with the busy buyer. He is not overworked either, but when a salesman calls, the salesman is confronted with a scene of such activity that he believes it hardly worth while mentioning the reason for his call. Remembering the axiom *never attempt to sell under adverse conditions*, the salesman excuses himself for interrupting the buyer while he is so busy, and leaves, with the buyer assuring him that he will see him some time later. But the salesman may have overlooked the extension of the axiom: *be sure that the conditions really* ARE *adverse. Don't jump to conclusions.*

It is so easy to believe that you are being confronted with an adverse selling situation when, in reality, the buyer is

(a) always on the go and, therefore, whenever you call the situation will be no different;

(b) going into his 'busy-buyer act' especially for your benefit.

Generally, the busy buyer doesn't use his act only as a

defence against salesmen. He just likes to give everyone the impression that he works twenty-four hours a day at top speed all the time, and if this enables him to get rid of unwelcome visitors, so much the better.

Look for these signs when meeting the busy buyer for the first time:

1. a constantly ringing telephone;
2. he tells you he must make a telephone call before the interview begins;
3. constant interruptions from his staff;
4. he examines papers while you are talking, mumbling something about always having to do two things at once;
5. he leaves the office saying, 'Excuse me, I've just got to see our maintenance engineer—be back in five minutes.'

There are two ways of tackling the busy buyer. He must be interested very quickly in the salesman's proposition, and that interest must be maintained. Also, the salesman must let the buyer know that he is impressed by the scene of activity.

The salesman might say,

'Mr White, how do you keep up this pace?'

This will give the buyer the opportunity of saying what his reasons are for being so busy: lack of staff, tremendous pressure of work; 'It's the way I'm built'. But while he is talking, the salesman will notice that he is beginning to slow down, because he is talking about one of his favourite subjects—himself. This will relax the busy buyer, who will enjoy impressing the salesman with his ability to do the work of three men. Once having established this point, the busy buyer is often prepared to sit back and listen to the salesman.

KNOW YOUR BUYERS

To understand the buyer is to understand yourself. Most of us at some time or another, have acted a part when buying.

Ask yourself these questions:

When I am in a shop, have I ever said, 'I have an appointment so I shall have to call back and try it on later'?

Or you may be looking at a piece of furniture in a shop, costing, perhaps, £250 but you only want to spend £50.

On such an occasion have you ever said to your wife, 'Well, it would go very well in our room, dear' when you haven't the slightest intention of paying £250 for that piece of furniture?

Or when your wife insists that you visit a showroom with her to look at a new refrigerator which you don't want her to buy, have you acted the part of the taciturn buyer, just answering her in monosyllables?

And when buying a car, have you shown off to the assistant by rattling off all you know about fuel injection systems, or double balancing shock absorbers?

You may not be able to identify yourself as having taken part in these scenes, but if you think hard enough you will remember occasions when you have been the too-busy buyer, the silent buyer, the stubborn or the talkative buyer.

When we understand the parts we play when considering a purchase, we shall more readily understand that professional buyers are no different from us. Some days they feel well; on others they are below par. Some days their responsibilities lie very heavily upon them, and this shows; while on other occasions, when everything is running smoothly in the factory, they will act differently towards you.

A professional salesman soon recognises all the signs and acts accordingly.

When you can recognise the parts the buyers play you will have taken your first step towards motivating them to listen and be interested in YOU.

6

Buyer Motivation

To be certain that his offer has the right appeal a salesman must understand the reasons behind a buying decision—what motivates a buyer to buy. Is it price—quality—confidence in a supplier? It could be any or all of these reasons, and selling would be easier if buying motives could be isolated so simply.

To understand motives it is easier to begin with fundamentals. Here are reasons, taken from biographies and autobiographies, which has motivated men to explore:

Explorer A: 1. *Main Motive:* To discover rare plant specimens.
             2. To discover his physiological and psychological limits.
             3. To test his endurance.

Explorer B: 1. *Main Motive:* To win the applause of others by conquering the unconquerable.
             2. To discover his self.

Explorer C: 1. *Main Motive:* To contest previous theories about the origin of a tribe of people.
             2. To write a book.

Explorer D: 1. *Main Motive:* Self enjoyment.
             2. To make a film for television so that others might share his enjoyment.

Explorer E: 1. *Main Motive:* To get away from a humdrum existence.
             2. To prove to family and friends that he was different from others.
             3. To seek a quiet existence.
             4. Revulsion against overcrowded modern cities.
             5. To find out if Robinson Crusoe could exist under present-day conditions on an uninhabited island.

On the face of it, the main objective of Explorer A was to seek rare plant specimens, but perhaps what finally convinced him that he should take risks financially and physically, was the need to test himself—to discover his physiological and psychological limits.

Explorer E yearned to get away from a humdrum existence, but he was also motivated by a need to achieve some inner peace in the security of life on an island, and to be unique amongst men.

The lessons to be learned from these examples of motivation are these:

1. There are usually a main motive and subsidiary motives behind every human action;

2. A motive which influences one person may not move another, although both may have dual objectives.

These facets of human behaviour, accepted by most anthropologists, psychologists, and scientists, have a direct application to decision makers.

1. Buyers, while usually having a main buying motive, are also swayed by subsidiary motives.

2. Buyers employed by different companies may buy the same product from the same supplier, but for different reasons.

Underlying Motives in Buying Decisions

One salesman may have a price advantage; another an efficiency advantage; a third a design advantage over competitors, but each may lose orders by thinking in terms only of motivating a buyer because of his one potential advantage. While a buyer might appear to be mainly interested in design, he could also be motivated by security (e.g. by a three-year guarantee). The salesman having efficiency as his advantage might not appreciate that the buyer could be influenced in his decision through fear (the shop stewards might not approve of the high speed efficiency of the equipment.) And the salesman who drives home the price advantage may not realise that health factors could deter a buyer (the equipment, although cheaper in price, unless carefully maintained could, perhaps, give off unhealthy fumes).

Each of these salesmen might well be able to cope with the buyer's need for security, fear, or concern for health, but overlook the need for emphasising these motives.

You may well ask the questions:

But if people are motivated to act in different ways to reach a similar objective, how can I know which main motivator to use in my sales offer? Also, how do I discover subsidiary motivators?

Here is a brief answer: (the subject is fully covered in the next chapter.)'

Regular calling will enable you to learn the motivators applying to individual buyers. You also learn by observation, by asking the buyer questions, and by listening to, and assessing, his replies. But you should include in your sales offer all the prime and subsidiary motivators applicable to your product or service. If a product or service has a different application for different buyers, it is perfectly feasible to use selective motivators.

The salesman's objective must always be to try to include in his sales offer the motivational force or forces which will impel the buyer to buy.

Buying Motives

A rational motive is one which is the result of reasoning. It stems from that part of the brain which is the powerhouse of rational thinking, the high cortex. Emotion stems from a lower part of the brain, yet continually, the high order of mental reasoning gives way to the lower order of emotional response. Over and over again, men's emotions take precedence over reason.

Rationally, the late Edward, Duke of Windsor, should not have given up his throne to marry a divorced woman. Emotionally, he could do no other than live with the woman he loved.

Rationally, a man should keep calm when faced with a situation which could lead to his dismissal. Emotionally, he might precipitate that dismissal by losing his temper.

What is all this about? you may ask. *Love of a woman—getting the sack—what help are these to an industrial salesman?*

Remember this fact:

Every known action has a motive behind it, and buyers, men or women, are human beings with human frailties.

When a managing director insists that a friend or client visit his factory to see a new piece of machinery or a modern conveyor belt system or a new computer, his main object is not to impress him with the instant statistics of the computer, or the fact that ten thousand knobs a second pass on to another phase in production instead of the previous seven thousand knobs. He shows his wares as a stamp collector shows his albums. He is proud of his purchase—therefore, *pride* could have played a part when the initial order was placed.

Although it may be rare for sentiment to play a part in industrial buying, it can happen. When a buyer purchases goods from Thomas & Son because he has been doing so for twenty-five years, it may be because these suppliers have always provided a fine service, but sentiment can also play its part—otherwise other suppliers would be tested on occasion.

A buyer will sometimes say, 'I've seen that firm grow over thirty-five years. I knew Bill Thomas's father very well.'

A salesman should be aware of *sentiment* as a buying reason, if only to work out ways of overcoming it and getting his share of that buyer's business.

It was emotional buying which took precedence during the Buy British drive some years ago. *Sentiment* for the old country was played upon. When a salesman says, 'We are a local firm and can give you quick service', indirectly he is attempting to motivate a buyer by a *sentimental* appeal. No salesman should ever say, 'You ought to buy from us because we are a local firm.' That is not playing on sentiment, but on charity.

One of the strongest of all emotional appeals is *the approval of others*. That pat on the back can mean as much to the owner of a small workshop as it does to a professional buyer or a managing director.

Every buyer delights in hearing:

You bought well.

That new fork-lift truck is first-class.

What a difference the new racking has made!

Your design group did a grand job.

You were very wise to change to leasing.

The professional salesman knows that, again and again, emotion plays a part in motivating a buyer to buy. Rover cars took full page advertisements in many papers to stress the safety factors of their cars. Heading the advertisement was a picture of a mother with her two children. The caption read: *Three important reasons why you should consider a Rover 2000 for your holiday.* The copy then began: *If you've got a wife and kids you must put safety at the top of your list.* Half-way down the page was a sub-caption: *And 23 reasons more.* Twenty-three safety factors were then listed. Few readers would study them carefully, but every reader got the message: *If I love my family I must buy a Rover.*

Rationally, all Rover needed to do in the advertisement was to state, one after the other, the twenty-three safety factors and that should have been sufficient to motivate many potential buyers. But Rovers made their main appeal an emotional one.

Classification of Buying Motives

rational	emotional
gain or saving of money	satisfaction of pride
satisfaction of caution	pleasure
benefit to health	sentimental reasons
protection and security	fear
utility value	envy
	approval of others
	social achievement
	to feel important

Here is a more specific classification of rational motives applicable to the industrial salesman:

Profit   direct gain of money—return from investment—cost reduction—increased output—less absenteeism.

Efficiency   overall performance—it is faster—*easier to handle—less risk of breakdown*—less complicated—more powerful—quieter in operation—works to finer limits.

Protection and Security	confidence in supplier—guaranteed standards—guaranteed deliveries—elimination of risk to employees—good after-sales service—wards off competition.
Appearance	good design—compact—modern in its concept—wide range of colours.
Durability	long life—less maintenance—withstands rough usage—*less risk of breakdowns*.
Utility	saving in time—labour—effort—more convenient to use—*easier to handle*.
Health	better working conditions—reduced strain—better environment—benefits employees (canteen food, air conditioning, lighting, etc.)

Because of his understanding of buyers' motivation, a salesman is able to build a strong sales offer—one which will appeal to the widest range of industrial buyers.

Problem-Solving Motivators

When a buyer has a problem he has worries, and no one likes worries. When a salesman is told of a problem, provided he knows the advice he may give will be within his company's policy, he should give high priority to his customers' interests.

When a buyer receives a stream of complaints because a component part keeps breaking down, he is a worried man. If his own R and D department cannot solve that problem, he probably lies awake at night thinking about it. When the experts try test after test, yet breakdowns still occur, it can be with real relief that that buyer hears from a salesman that his company might be able to help.

This may seem unusual in industry, but it happens time and time again. If that salesman solves the problem he is IN. He has given the buyer PROTECTION and SECURITY. He has also benefited the buyer's HEALTH. That buyer, in the future, will always give the salesman a warm welcome, and orders if possible.

When the managing director is complaining bitterly of

rising costs, or is showing his concern at low output, he will listen intently to the salesman who can help to solve his problem.

It could be that a new machine is required, but its size would need a different factory layout. The salesman of the machine could, perhaps, help to solve the layout problem as well. (Motivation, PROFIT.)

Or it might be that delivery costs are getting out of hand, a problem which could be solved by a well-qualified salesman selling a specialised delivery service. Perhaps there is a cash problem—liquidity. The salesman selling a leasing service—equipment, plant, computers—could help solve this problem by showing how capital can be used more efficiently. (Motivation, EFFICIENCY.)

All industrial salesmen must remind themselves continually that a prime motivator is to help a buyer to solve his problems. There are other, quite dissimilar problems, which buyers have to deal with, and which salesmen can help them to resolve.

The professional salesman knows that he is not only in direct competition with competitors, but also with the day to day demand made upon buyers—demands from associates and employees.

No company, however large, can afford to buy everything offered to them—more luxurious offices—a head office in the centre of town—a private executive aircraft—a larger canteen—more sophisticated computers—bigger cars for salesmen—an exhibition yacht. And no managing director can agree to all the demands made of him by the various departments in his organisation.

A managing director has to withstand this type of pressure continually. Research and development may want new testing equipment—the works manager cannot do without new paint spraying booths—the production manager must have that new expensive, all-purpose piece of machinery—the despatch manager wants more lorries—while the warehouse manager wants extra space built on to his warehouse. The PRO, conscious of the company image, wants a landscape gardener to lay out the fields in front of the factory. The financial director needs a highly sophisticated accounting machine—and on the factory floor the cleaner wants new brooms and the canteen manager needs more cutlery.

The salesman calling on that company has to compete for the firm's cash. He has to make that managing director (or his buyer) give his product or service priority over the accounting machine, the garden layout, the paint spraying booths. How, then, can a salesman use his knowledge of motivators to persuade a buyer to give his product or service this priority?

The answer is: By creating a *want* in the mind of the buyer.

Creating Wants

There are specific areas in which a salesman can create the right atmosphere for a buyer to *want* the products or services he is offering. Even a specifying authority—architect, consulting engineer, welfare officer—will only make a decision when he or she *wants* to favour one supplier instead of another.

Understanding motivational forces allows a salesman to create a desire to buy by appealing to a buyer's *wants*. And what we all *want* when we buy are benefits to ourselves, our families, or our company. There is no one point in a sale when desire is created, any more than there is one time only when confidence is established. A salesman is always building confidence in himself and his company—and every time he shows a buyer a benefit he should be creating a *want*. The salesman who builds benefit after benefit is the professional, who gets more than his 'share of the business'.

While most minds are influenced by emotional motivators, all benefits are based on rational motivators.

Understanding motivational forces allows a salesman to concentrate on the main benefits which appeal to a particular buyer.

Buyer A is mainly motivated by profitability.

Buyer B is mainly motivated by security.

Buyer C is mainly motivated by efficiency.

Salesman Jones will show Buyer A the benefit of profitability to be derived from his product or service, and will bring this benefit up again and again. Salesman Brown, selling to Buyer B, will concentrate on proving the benefits of regular deliveries, twenty-four hour service and standards maintained. Salesman White, selling to Buyer C, demonstrates that the efficiency of his product must benefit the buyer's production line.

The professional salesman, while concentrating on the main benefits offered by his product or service will, however, never overlook all the subsidiary benefits. It is often these subsidiary benefits which will finally motivate a buyer to buy.

Salesmen also create *wants* by talking in terms of what a product *does* rather than what it *is*.

Do you buy a mattress because the salesman tells you that 'There is a cushioning of fleece on one side of the mattress and white cotton felt on the other'? Or do you buy because the professional salesman has told you that 'With this mattress you will feel extra warm in the winter, and cool in summer'?

Does a buyer buy because the salesman, steeped in technicalities, says, 'This melamine-formaldehyde resin, when used in admixture with alkyd resins, gives a much faster heat cure than a urea formaldehyde resin used alone. The outstanding characteristics which urea resins supply to films are further enhanced with melamine resins which are then resistant to various chemical re-agents and maintain durability and colour retention to heat and light'? Or does he buy because the professional salesman has said, 'The melamine-formaldehyde resin is used with alkyd resins, so that you will be able to produce a porcelain-like appearance, resistant to abrasions and heat'?

Does a buyer buy because a salesman says, 'We cut the core iron plates to have mitred joints so accurate that the flux path has a minimum distortion . . .'? Or does he buy because the professional salesman says, 'Your running costs for iron losses will be cut to a minimum . . .'?

Buyers buy for the latter reasons—those given by the professional salesman who, while briefly showing the technicalities as facts, never over-elaborates them and always translates them into direct benefits to the buyer or his company.

Here are examples of *wants* created by personalising the benefits: The salesman does not say:

'Our new machine is fitted with a double size platen.'

He does say:

> *'You can print two pages together and halve the cost because of the new double size platen in our machine.'*

He does not say:

'Our Plutos bearings have higher load capacity and longer life.'

He does say:

> *'You can save money, because the higher load capacities of Plutos bearings means that you can use a smaller, less expensive unit.'*

Motivation by Filling Needs and Stimulating Wants

In every industry there are basic needs catered for by a host of suppliers of raw materials, component parts, standard tools, packaging supplies and so on. These needs can be counted by the hundred in some factories, by the thousand in others. Suppliers of basic needs are usually in a highly competitive market. Every week a buyer will see salesmen eager to tell him why he should buy from them instead of from his current suppliers of disinfectants or ball bearings; cleaning materials or switchgear; overalls or electric motors.

What motivates a buyer to change suppliers, or agree to a change in the specification of the product he is buying regularly from one of his suppliers? He will only change his mind if there will be additional benefits from switching to a new supplier or agreeing to changes in specification.

To change the mind of a buyer a salesman must, therefore, turn a basic need into a *want*—a *want* for his product or service. As the main buying benefit is usually already obtainable from the present supplier, the salesman who is competing to fill a basic need must be sure of selling every subsidiary benefit offered by his product. One of these could be the motivator to change a basic need into a *want* for his product.

Unrecognised or Real Needs

An *unrecognised need*, usually referred to as the *real need*, is sometimes obvious, sometimes not. For example, before domestic refrigerators were on the market, although block ice was often used to keep food cool, the majority of households kept food in cellars, food safes, or standing in bowls of water. As far as the people of those times were concerned, their need was being filled. The food was just that shade cooler, lasted just that little longer than if it were left in an outside warmer atmosphere, so these simple methods filled the need. When, eventually, household refrigerators were marketed, which filled the *real need*, there was a great deal of resistance to buying. Housewives believed that except, perhaps, in very hot weather, they had no food deterioration problems, and were content with their food safes, etc. Salesmen who sold refrigerators in those days had a very difficult job persuading people to *want* a refrigerator, because the housewives did not recognise their *real need*.

The recognising of *real needs* is not confined to the householder; skilled buyers, brilliant managing directors, heads of production units, often do not recognise their *real needs*. Photocopying machines are now looked upon by most businesses as essential office equipment—yet when they were first launched on the market they met with extreme resistance. It was not until salesmen employed by the Rank Xerox organisation were able to *create the want* by showing the *real need* that photocopying made headway. Nowadays, as new photocopiers come on to the market, salesmen have to find those *extra benefits* to enable them to compete with the market leaders.

A managing director may believe that his *basic need* is satisfied by an outsize card index filing system—a system which has grown over the years, entailing the use of many filing cabinets, and causing overcrowding in the offices.

'We shall have to move,' says the office manager.

'Yes,' agrees the managing director, 'I think it is coming to that.'

But his *real need* could be for a micro-film system installation. Such an installation would save a great deal of space and, retrieval taking only seconds, would enable staff who have constantly to search the files for information to be better employed. The filing cabinets could be disposed of, and there would be an improved service both to customers and salesmen.

The need being unrecognised, a salesman selling micro-film systems would have to emphasise these and other benefits, until the *want* was created.

Here is an example from Nu-aire (Contracts) Ltd, a company within our own group, which saw that a whole dimension in building design could be opened up if a certain product were made available. The building industry did not, at first, recognise the *need*.

British building regulations state that a toilet/bathroom must be provided either with a window which can be opened, or with a mechanical extractor system which changes the air in the room a specified number of times in the hour. Also, various local requirements specify that the fan system serving these internal rooms must be of the standby type, so that should the fan fail, the reserve fan automatically takes over. All these rules are designed to protect the health of tenants, and are strictly enforced both by the public health inspector and by the building inspectorate.

Until about 1967 the need for ventilation had been met by special fans designed to service internal bathrooms and WCs. They were limited to sizes suitable for a number of rooms linked together by a common duct system and therefore, the only occasions on which internal bathrooms and WCs were used were in fairly high rise buildings. Because of this situation, low and medium rise buildings were not designed with internal bathrooms and WCs. On the other hand, there were quite obvious pressures on the building industry to bring these rooms into the internal core of the construction. These reasons were:

1. Lack of suitable building land and its cost made narrow frontage dwellings attractive to the developers and architects;
2. The grouping together of all services in the central core reduced costs.

Nu-aire (Contracts) Ltd recognised a *need*, and designed a

range of small units suitable for ventilating individual internal bathrooms and WCs. They satisfied the various standards, were inexpensive, and most important, they could be selected and detailed by the architect without help from specialised service engineers.

After the *real need* was explained by Nu-aire salesmen, the demand was created. These units subsequently directly influenced architecture in this country, so that today, internal bathrooms/WCs are a feature of dwellings, from low to high rise types; but in spite of the uniqueness of these units, Nu-aire salesmen, time and time again, had to make the *need* for the units recognised, and then *create the want*.

BUYER MOTIVATION

To summarise, here are the steps to an appreciation of buyer motivation:

1. There is a motive behind every human action.
2. There is always a prime motive and a subsidiary motive. The salesman, while concentrating on the prime motive, must never overlook the subsidiary motives.
3. Different buyers buy similar equipment, but often for different reasons. Selective motives should be used, when applicable.
4. There are rational and emotional buying motives, and the importance of emotional motives must never be underrated.
5. The salesman's objective must always be to try to include in his sales offer the motivational force or forces which will impel the buyer to buy.
6. Buyers first fulfil *basic needs*, but often do not *recognise* their *real needs*.
7. Benefits should be 'personalised'.
8. A salesman turns *needs* into *wants* by proving benefits to the buyer or his company.

BENEFITS

Understanding buyer motivation means appreciating why and how he arrives at his decisions—why a buyer has a fear of change. And most important, it enables a salesman to *progress an interview*; this means that while he is actually selling he will know—not by intuition but by sheer logic—how a buyer will react to claims, statements, offers; and he will know the underlying thoughts of the buyer when objections are raised.

The professional salesman also knows that it is BENEFITS *derived from a knowledge of buyer motivation which act as a stimulus, and develop a* WANT *in the mind of the buyer.*

7

Obtaining the Interview

It is wise to be armed with every scrap of information that can help you to close an order. It is right to plan your sales offer. It is correct to check your sales kit before a call. But these preparations are wasted if a prospective buyer won't see you. Interviews can be hard to get when a buyer is well guarded.

Managing directors, works managers, project managers, purchasing personnel, advertising managers, are usually in their offices or workshops, and between them and the salesman are assistants, secretaries, receptionists, and commissionaires—all ready to bar the way.

Whether a salesman is seen by a buyer largely depends on the buyer's need for the product or service being offered. Salesmen selling repeat products usually have no problem getting interviews, but salesmen selling capital goods or services, or trying to open new accounts for component parts etc., often waste valuable time endeavouring to be seen when they should be selling.

Appointments by Telephone

How can a salesman get the maximum number of interviews? What are his alternatives? He can call cold or make an appointment by telephone.

Even if he is given inquiries to follow up he will more often than not have to telephone for an appointment. Cold calling or prospecting, as it is sometimes termed, will always have its place in some forms of selling, but it is usually a fill-in for the industrial salesman. Rather than waste time between appointments he will call cold on any near-by prospects, but prospecting as a planned system of working can be very time-consuming. For example, there can be long waits in reception areas until the buyer is disengaged. Also, a full day's work may result in only two good interviews. But telephoning in advance may enable a salesman to make four or five appointments a day.

Preparation

The basis of all telephone selling—and making appointments by telephone is hard selling—must be good preparation. There are several rules to follow before making an appointment by telephone, and one golden rule: *you must find out the prospect's name.*

Knowing the prospect's name will help you to handle his telephone operator, and by addressing the buyer by name you are able to bring immediate warmth to the relationship.

When you telephone, remember:

1. You must have customer files or information cards available. This information allows you to anticipate a customer or prospect's questions, or his objections to giving an interview. A customer may have had a delivery complaint. A prospect might not have purchased from you previously because he considered your prices too high. With this knowledge available you can forestall his queries.

2. Directories, brochures, and any other information which you may need should be at hand. The names and telephone numbers of calls you intend making should be listed in front of you and, of course, pen and paper available for making notes.

3. Your diary is invaluable to you. Whenever possible you will suggest days and times for appointments to suit *your* convenience. Your aim must be to fill the day with appointments.

4. Make sure that you will not be disturbed while telephoning.

5. Never ask a secretary or telephone operator to get the buyer on the line for you. Always dial direct yourself.

Now, are you ready? Let us assume that your name is White, and that you are calling on a production director, Mr Smith. Although you want to speak to him personally, you must *never* make a misleading statement to obtain your objective.

Making a call

Pick up the telephone, dial the number, and on being greeted by the telephone operator, ask to speak to Mr Smith.

One of three things can happen:

1. The operator will transfer you immediately to Mr Smith, and all will be well.

2. The operator will ask you your business.

3. The operator may put you through to Mr Smith's secretary. To avoid 1 and 2 you must use an authoritative approach.

> 'Will you please tell Mr Smith your production manager that John White is on the line for him. Thank you.'

The *John* personalises the approach. Never use the prefix Mr. The *thank you* gives it a finality which does not invite a response. Unless the telephone operator has special screening instructions regarding incoming calls you will be put through to Mr Smith.

Now we come to 2. The operator asks you for further information. You answer, quite simply:

> 'It's a business matter.'

Don't add anything further. It is not a misleading statement, because it is a business matter (not a personal call) which you can discuss only with Mr Smith, the production director.

Alternatively, it will show equal authority if you imply that you wish to discuss something of importance which must, of course, be truthful and relative to your proposition. For example:

> 'It is in connection with Mr Smith's new factory.'

There is another excellent approach if a letter has been sent in advance to the buyer. You can then say:

> 'It is with reference to the letter I wrote him . . .'

If, however, the operator has been instructed to insist on obtaining information from every caller asking for Mr Smith, you should say:

> 'I'm sorry, but it is a very involved matter. I think it might be best if you put me through to Mr Smith's secretary.'

It is sometimes advisable when making appointments to ask for a secretary in the first place, but in the main it is better to ask for the executive concerned. The secretary might be away or out of her office, and in this event the operator *may* put you straight through to the man you want to contact.

If you speak to the secretary, however, either by your own

request or because the operator has instructions, you will then have the selling task of persuading her to make an appointment for you to see Mr Smith.

You will use the golden words:

'*I should like to ask your advice*. I want to see Mr Smith because . . .'

You will not win every time, but you will win far more often than you will lose. In the majority of cases you will, therefore, be able to speak to Mr Smith.

What do you say to him?

The Hinge

There should, whenever possible, be a hinge on which to hang your approach. This can be a letter which you or your company have written, an advertisement, a new product—a special claim you can make for your product—or a reference from a friend or business associate. Your approach could be:

'Mr Smith, this is John White of the Bridgewater Machine Tool Company. Have you a moment to speak on the telephone?'

This courteous request, 'Have you a moment . . .' is not laid down as a fixed rule. It can, however, be very effective. It relaxes the prospect, because you have only asked him for a moment of his time. Also, it shows a courtesy that is lacking in so many telephone calls.

Whether you use this sentence or not, you must now repeat the prospect's name, after you have given him the name of your company.

Letter Hinge

'Mr Smith, did you receive my letter?'

'No, what was it about?'

'Mr Smith, it was about your . . .'

Another example:

'Mr Smith, did you receive my letter?'

'About your new lathes, wasn't it?'

'That's right, I would like to call to see you to explain . . .'

Reference Hinge

> 'Mr Smith, we haven't met, but John Williams asked me to contact you.'

You then have to sell Mr Smith the idea that you are worth seeing.

Question Hinge

When you haven't a hinge of any kind, ask a question:

> 'Mr Smith, this is Mike Boon of the Bessing Group—have you heard of our organisation?'

Whether you receive the reply 'Yes' or 'No' is immaterial, because it will take you smoothly into the main reason for your call.

The Quick Approach Close

In all forms of selling it is axiomatic that a salesman should think of the close as soon as the sale begins, but in telephone selling there is a difference. You can actually close at the approach. The buyer might be influenced by the name of your company, or interested in the product or service you are selling, or he may like the sound of your voice—you sound like someone he should listen to—or it may even be that he is very busy and arrives at a quick decision. Whatever the reason, this form of approach does get appointments. This is how to do it:

With conviction in your voice to create the impression that there cannot be a refusal you say:

> 'Good morning, Mr Jones. This is Jack Smith of Halliday Publications. I should like to take up just eight minutes of your time to tell you. about our new journal for your industry and its wonderful advertising pull. Would Wednesday morning or Wednesday afternoon be more convenient for me to call?'

This approach covers a lot of ground. It is brief; it asks for only a short interview; it states your business; and it closes.

Be Special

A wonderful word to use in all approaches is *special*, or *specially*—

> 'Mr Smith, I am calling you *specially* to tell you about . . .'

'Mr Jones, there is a *special* reason why I should like to see you.'

Keep to the Rules

Although the quick close will get you interviews, in many cases there will be a request for further information.

Here are some points to remember:

Time is not on your side, so keep the benefit short.

You must not become involved in a full sales offer.

Keep the objective in mind: *to obtain an interview.*

You must use short sentences.

You must use understandable words.

You must be authoritative, but must never talk down to the buyer.

You must not try to be too clever. You have to persuade the buyer that you are a sincere person by the words you use, and by the tone of your voice.

You must have a reason for not giving full information over the telephone, e.g. samples to be shown, a model of a building to examine, figures to analyse, a drawing to discuss, or matters so personal that they should be discussed face to face.

The Main Benefit

You must stake your claim for an interview in a few compelling words:

'I'd like to show you some recent information on . . .'

'You will want to consider six ideas for cutting down overheads in your offices.'

'We have designed a very unusual saving plan which will be of great benefit to you.'

'The Mighty Midget office copier is no bigger than your desk pad. Knowing something of your company's activities, I know you would find this of tremendous help for personal use . . .'

'You will want to handle the stitcher yourself, to see how well it works.'

Your aim is to intrigue the prospect, to interest him so that he will want to hear more and will give you an interview.

The Objections

What could his objections be? He can hardly object to your product or service, because you have only given him the barest outline. He can only object to you taking up his time at an interview.

He can answer, 'I'll see you,' and all will be well.
Or,

> 'Send me the information.'
> 'Tell me now.'
> 'I'm too busy.'

There are several ways of tackling the request for further information.

> 'Mr Smith, you would want to see proof of how a company has been able to increase overall production by up to 28 %.'
> 'What I want to talk to you about, Mr Brown, is details of a new way in which you can protect your money and beat inflation. Would next Tuesday morning . . .?'
> 'Mr Jones, you demand a very fast delivery service. We can provide that at low cost, and you will want to examine this claim. It is for this reason that I want the opportunity of meeting you. May I call on . . .?'
> 'I cannot advise you, Mr Black, until I know one or two things about your company.'
> 'You would need to look at our analysis forms, Mr Clark, I'll bring them with me. It will only take a few minutes— may I call on . . .?'

To the statement, 'I am too busy' the salesman has several answers, according to what he is selling.

> 'That is why I am telephoning you, Mr Smith, because I know you are so busy. I can help you in this direction by cutting down some of the demands on your time.'

Ego building can also be sound policy:

> 'Mr White, I have found that it is the busy people like you who are interested . . .'

Or assume that the prospect is only encountering a temporary rush of business:

> 'Of course, Mr Howell, I know how busy you are, I was not thinking of disturbing you today or tomorrow. Will you be able to see me on Thursday or Friday of next week?'

If you reach a point where you feel you are antagonising the prospect, then you must never shut the door to a future appointment.

> 'I'll call you again in a fortnight's time, Mr Smith.'

If this does not work there is always one final request that you can make. It is rarely refused:

> 'Mr Smith, there are some times of the day when you are not so busy as others, although I appreciate that you cannot specify them. When I am near your offices, may I call on the off-chance of seeing you?'

He will nearly always say 'Yes' and this is noted in your prospecting diary.

Following the telephone call, after two or three visits at the most, you will find that you will be able to see Mr Smith.

The Close

Tying up an appointment is different from locking up an order, when you can use any of the closes set out in the sales presentation. This is not possible when selling the interview. Nearly always, therefore, you will use the Alternative Close, based on an appointment time.

Most salesmen suggest a time for a meeting on the hour or the half-hour. You can be different. Put forward 9.10 a.m. or 3.50 p.m. The very unexpected nature of this suggestion will often bring its own reward, but the main reason for using this technique is that many busy people make appointments on the hour or half-hour, some of which will last for the full period, while others will be cut short. The odd time, therefore, will often appeal to the prospect whose appointments on the hour may leave him periods in between which are free.

Remember, you are only asking for a few minutes of his time, knowing that if you interest him he will ask you to stay.

The close can, therefore, be:

'Will Wednesday or Thursday suit you best, Mr Lovell?'

'Er—Wednesday.'

'Morning, or afternoon?'

'Afternoon is best for me.'

'That's fine, Mr Lovell. Can you make it two-ten? Or would four-fifty be more convenient?'

'Ten past two would suit me.'

'Thank you, Mr Lovell, I look forward to being with you at ten past two on Wednesday.'

Example:

(The salesman of Arrow Weighing Machine Company is telephoning a works director seeking an appointment.)

'Mr Harvey? Good morning, this is Peter Lisle of The Arrow Weighing Machine Company. We met some three years ago when the maintenance contract on your weighing equipment was arranged. Can you spare me a moment?' Yes.'

'Mr Harvey, the contract is due for renewal next month. You will want to see the new proposal—may I call on Wednesday?'

'There's no need for you to come here. You can post the papers on to me.'

'Thank you, Mr Harvey, but reports from my engineers show that certain machines are being used either less or more than they were three years ago. You will agree that we should try to get the frequency of maintenance on each machine in relation to its use and importance. On Wednesday I can explain.'

'You'd better talk to my chief engineer about this. He'll know what he wants, and I will accept his recommendations, provided the charge for the contract isn't any higher than before. Costs seem to keep rising.'

'They do indeed, Mr Harvey, and you will understand that in providing a service a very high proportion of the premium is directly related to labour costs—and we both know how wages keep going up. In any event, you and I can work this out between us, and I'm sure you'll agree that we should have a talk about it. Would Wednesday...?'

Particular Points

1. Reason for call made clear. Mr Harvey *might* have agreed to see the salesman without more discussion.
2. A valid, although secondary reason for wanting an appointment.
3. The primary reason comes out, but is not dealt with as Peter Lisle does not want to become involved in a price discussion. The need for the meeting is brought to a 'you and I' situation. Lisle has raised the importance of the issue, and has built up the ego of Mr Harvey.

Conclusion

To succeed in obtaining more appointments by telephone you must:

> know your prospects and their business;
> have a definite reason for asking for the interview;
> have a planned approach;
> have a main benefit to stress the need for the appointment;
> be prepared to listen, and don't pounce. (It might be that the prospect is about to give you an interview when you interrupt.)
> smile when you talk on the telephone;
> talk a little slower than usual?
> if not making headway, ask questions;
> sound enthusiastic. Your enthusiasm will vibrate over the wires and will do more than anything else to get that appointment for you.

The obtaining of appointments is a challenge to all salesmen —a challenge which, if accepted, can lead to a far greater volume of business.

Prospecting

Visiting cards have their uses when calling on customers. A buyer who sees many salesmen cannot be expected to remember every name, but if he has the visiting card before him, sent in by the receptionist, he can refresh his mind by glancing at it. Sometimes a buyer asks for a card. Rather than apologise for not having one, carry a card. Also, if you can always get an appointment by sending through your card, then keep a good supply always available. But if you have frequently called on a buyer, each time sending up your card, and each time failing in your mission, you must work to a different plan.

The card might show the name of a company—Johnson's Tools Ltd for example. A buyer glances at it, and being satisfied with his present suppliers, returns it with the message, 'Nothing today'. But the salesman representing Johnson's Tools Ltd, might have a special tool which would interest that buyer; this information cannot be learned from the card.

Thousands of salesmen make thousands of abortive calls because they persist in using cards for the wrong reasons.

Here is a technique which usually brings about interviews.

If a reception office is guarded by a telephonist it is essential that you walk briskly up to the reception desk. If you have a hangdog look, or appear ill-at-ease, you won't succeed even in the first part of your task, which is to convey a sense of the importance of your visit to the receptionist.

You smile and say, 'Good morning, will you please tell Mr Brown that Tim Heyworth is here to see him.' Spell your name—'H-e-y-w-o-r-t-h.' Then look away, as if preoccupied with thoughts of great moment.

If you indicate that you expect to be questioned by her she will, invariably, ask, 'What is your business?'

In most cases she will telephone Mr Brown and tell him that Mr Tim Heyworth is in the waiting-room to see him. Mr Brown then has two choices: He can ask the telephonist, 'Will you please find out what he wants?' or he can say, 'Tell him to come up and see me.'

If, however, in spite of your looking away, the receptionist asks for information, you must give it. If, when telephoning Mr Brown she says, 'Mr Brown has asked the reason for your visit', try to answer Mr Brown's question yourself. You need only say, 'May I just have a word with him?' Now it is up to you to convince Mr Brown that he should see you.

Here are rules to remember for obtaining more interviews:

1. Treat receptionists with respect to obtain their co-operation.
2. Don't wait about too long—your time is valuable. If someone is going to keep you waiting for thirty or forty minutes it may pay you better to make a call elsewhere.
3. If there is any reading matter relating to the firm's activities in the reception office, study it while you are waiting.
4. If you are kept waiting a little while, don't keep worrying the receptionist.
5. When a secretary comes into the waiting-room, don't forget to stand up. And she will appreciate words like, 'I should be grateful for your help', or, 'I wonder if you can help me.' Most people like to help others.

8

Planning the Call

In industrial selling, the salesman who knows the precise needs of a buyer begins with a great advantage. Armed with the knowledge that his company has the resources to fill that need, he can readily create the *want* for his product or service.

A salesman, therefore, besides being a combination of communicator, public relations officer, teacher, adviser, problem solver, and information officer, has also to be part explorer, part detective. For example, before calling he has to discover if a company is a member of a group; if so, what facilities do the associated companies offer?

Only a salesman can fathom out the intricacies of a company's buying chain. Only a salesman can learn of components which may be required for a project at some future time. Only a salesman can discover quickly any change in a company's production methods, its involvement in new processes, or the expansion of its factory building.

It is certainly not true of the industrial salesman that his only valuable time is that spent in front of a buyer. He may make an exploratory call to find out who are the decision makers or the decision influencers—what competitive equipment is being used —what are the buyer's main needs. A salesman can never cease seeking information which will help him to carry negotiations to a successful conclusion. For example:

Does the company manufacture to British standards?
Does the company have to comply with overseas standards? (Some of these are much stricter than those applying in this country.)
Is the buyer closely tied to a large buying group? (e.g. manufacturing companies supplying direct mail houses and such firms as Marks & Spencer.)
Because of its need for long-term planning, is a company

tied to a competitor for some time ahead? (How long—one year? Two years?)

Is the business obtainable from the company too small to justify too much time spent in servicing the account?

Has a company potential growth and, therefore, is it worth nursing for future business?

Does the company have a list of approved suppliers? If so, what conditions have to be complied with to enable his company's name to be placed on that list?

The Planners

Salesmen can be placed roughly (very roughly) in three categories:

the meticulous planner
the constant planner
the semi-planner.

Even the most unprofessional salesman will do some pre-call planning, if it is only giving thought to the name of the buyer, or where he should park his car.

The *meticulous planner*, however, plans carefully each evening, firstly completing his report, then entering its details in a card index. Next he considers his work for the following day—what time should he spend telephoning to get appointments? Or if his appointments are already made, how long should he spend with each buyer? What are their needs? And so on . . .

The *constant planner* is nearly always an enthusiast, deeply concerned with every aspect of his job. He is continually planning—thinking ahead. When the late Ian Fleming was asked, 'When do you plan the writing of a book?' he answered 'All the time.' This statement is true of most authors. They are always delving into their minds to solve problems, to think of improvements for the next chapter, to re-plan a chapter already written, to consider the best approach to a publisher or to weigh up the film rights.

These thoughts pass through their mind while motoring or taking the dog for a walk, pretending to listen to the gossip of their wives or to the tittle-tattle of a cocktail party.

The author is no different from the salesman who is a *constant planner*. Except for report writing he does not necessarily set aside a special time for planning, because he is always planning, always jotting down notes.

Unfortunately, many a salesman is a *semi-planner*, believing that he can *play it by ear*. He doesn't bother to keep a card index, relying on his memory to bring back to his mind details of customers' requirements—names of decision influencers . . .

An example of the difference between the *meticulous planner* and the *semi-planner* is that the first will always carry coins with him for use in a public telephone. The *semi-planner* would never dream of checking whether he had the coins in his pocket each morning, and sometimes has to make this excuse to a customer 'I'm so sorry I'm late, but my car broke down and I didn't have a coin for the 'phone box. Believe it or not, I couldn't find a single passer-by who had change.'

The *semi-planner* is a muddler, who only does well if he is an outstandingly good salesman.

There are three stages in planning:
1. At regular intervals throughout a year.
2. Once a week.
3. Daily.

PLANNING AT REGULAR INTERVALS THROUGHOUT THE YEAR

Business is ever-changing; facts, and information given to a salesman, alter continuously. This necessitates a continuous reassessment of:

> product knowledge
> competitors and their products.

A salesman must also remind himself of the special features of his product or service at least once a month. Familiarity with a product can lead to a mental blockage, or to mental laziness. If these mental aberrations are not checked, orders can be lost.

A buyer on the friendliest of terms with a salesman can say this:

'I didn't know you *also* supplied hoses—I've given the
order to . . .'

Buyers often buy from competitors because they don't know
the full extent of the range of equipment of a trusted and regular
supplier. A buyer is also apt to forget special features, and
unless reminded of them will say:

'I didn't know your units could be adapted to a central
system—I thought you only made them for individual use.
I've given the order to . . .'

If a salesman doesn't remind himself constantly of those
features which helped him to get the order initially, he can lose
repeat business.

Reminders are an essential part of preparation.

WEEKLY PLANNING

A name sometimes given to weekly planning is *armchair planning*.
This conjures up visions of the salesman at home, seated in his
armchair, the children having been warned off, deep in
thought as he draws slowly on a cigarette, his mind acutely
alert. He is thinking ahead, planning his close.

A very nice and comforting picture, but most salesmen would
find it extremely difficult to arrange to have that kind of peace
on a Saturday or Sunday. All *armchair planning* really means is
taking 'time off' to deliberate and work out strategies for the week
ahead. Maybe this does take place when the family have gone
to bed, or before embarking on a Sunday morning picnic. Some-
how, time has to be found, unless you are a constant planner.
But even the constant planner needs to set aside some time to
consider more carefully the notes he has made during the week.

Armchair planning should be on these lines:

1. Read local papers, trade magazines, and technical and
financial news in national newspapers. Although a salesman
may have no interest in the stock market, p/e ratios, discounting,
or commodity prices, he will often find in the newspapers and
weekly journals which give prominence to the financial affairs of
companies a great deal of useful information. New business can

be obtained by salesmen after they have read a chairman's annual report, an analysis of a company by a city editor, or an account of a journey overseas by an export director.

Regional newspapers can also provide news of local companies' interest, while the trade and technical press should always be studied if only to enable a salesman to keep up to date with competitors' prices and services.

2. If possible, a salesman should regularly study the market potential for his product, so that he knows how his sales compare with those of his competitors. This is a salutary exercise which allows him to see his results in their true perspective. He can then plan accordingly.

No one likes to be beaten by a competitor. More important, figures can prove to a self-satisfied salesman that there is room for improvement.

3. Planning the week's work is essential. Good planning of territory coverage can mean an extra call; one additional call a week adds up to over forty-five extra calls a year. A salesman, when making his calling plans, should think of alternative calls which might have to be made. For example, his appointments might be:

Monday	9 a.m.	Call on A
	10.30 a.m.	Call on B
	11.30 a.m.	Call on C

But when he arrives at the premises of C he may find that the buyer has been called away unexpectedly. Therefore, when planning, he should consider the possibility of prospecting in C's area.

Routes to customers should also be carefully planned, to save time; parking places should be pinpointed.

4. Customer cards for those customers to be called upon during the following week should be extracted from the card index.

DAILY PLANNING

Although customer and prospect cards are checked at week-ends, it is wiser to study each evening those relevant to the following day's work. Daily planning is, in the main, a study of customers and prospective customers. The salesman will want to be reminded:

1. What a company manufactures.

   If any new products have been introduced.

   If they have made known any future plans.

2. If anything has been sold to that company previously, in which case details should be available.

   If there has been any complaint about the product or after-sales service.

   If the company may be supplied. It is not unusual for a salesman to take an order only to find that a stop has been put on that particular account. This could be because payments are in arrears, or more usually, because it has not been possible to get extra insurance cover for them against bad debts.

   If the company are prospective customers, which of the salesman's products will, in the main, interest the buyer.

   If there are any quotations outstanding, what competitors' products the company are using.

3. Who has authority to buy.

   Who could influence a buying decision.

4. Facts about a buyer and his interests.

5. Details of points discussed at a previous call.

6. Opportunities for future business.

7. Buyer's main needs.

8. The main objective of the call.

9. The secondary objective.

Demonstration Units and Sales Kits

The salesman must plan the order in which he will demonstrate the use of his equipment or use his sales aids. Too often a salesman giving a demonstration says,

> 'I'm sorry it's so dirty, but I only collected it late last night from . . .'
>
> 'It isn't perfect, but it's the best I can get.'
>
> 'It worked all right yesterday.'
>
> 'Have you a screwdriver?'

'These damned links have jammed!'

All equipment used for demonstration purposes must be checked over every evening, and possibly re-checked the following morning and checked again immediately after use. This is an essential part of planning.

Never risk losing a buyer's confidence by demonstrating with equipment which could be faulty. Rather put off the demonstration until perfect units are available. Similarly, a sales kit must be checked to be certain there are no dog-eared or stained leaflets, indecipherable drawings, or out-of-date figures.

Fashions in men's appearance change. Hair may be longer or shorter, trousers wider or narrower, shirts spotted or striped, faces shaven or bearded, but a sales kit must *always* be the same—immaculate.

Sales literature and sales aids should always be placed in the briefcase in the same order. This enables the salesman to extract the appropriate leaflet or catalogue without looking away from the buyer.

The objective of sales planning is to be prepared for every eventuality. Sales planning ensures that you give your buyer or prospective buyer the best possible service.

9

Offer Analysis

Carlyle wrote: *Let him who would move and convince others be first moved to convince himself.*

A salesman must be able to prove to himself that he is selling the right product, and offer analysis provides that proof, enabling him to identify *all* product features, and derive from them every single buyer benefit. It is the accumulation of these benefits which give proof of the value of the product.

To analyse, the dictionary informs us, is:

> To take to pieces; resolve into its constituent elements; to examine minutely; to examine critically.

To be able to offer a buyer every conceivable benefit, a salesman rarely has to take his product to pieces, but he will certainly have to examine it minutely, and critically.

But it isn't enough to analyse a product alone. The analysis must embrace every factor which could influence a favourable decision.

For example, what will create buyer confidence?

Confidence building can be likened to British invisible exports (royalties, commissions, finance, insurance, etc.). They cannot be seen leaving the ports, but without them the trade balance would be so far into the red that countries all over the world would lose confidence in our ability to meet our commitments.

A buyer cannot see (in advance of purchasing) honesty, a fair deal, the backing given to guarantees (what is a guarantee worth if a company goes bankrupt?); completion of work on time; help during periods of shortages; rapid service. Unless a customer believes that some or all of these benefits exist, he may decide to buy from one of his regular suppliers.

The Small Company

The salesman joining a newly formed or small company will

soon appreciate the need for confidence builders. Prospects may voice their fears by saying, 'Where are these in use? We have to be assured of continuity of supplies', or, 'I am not opening any new accounts.'

To overcome these fears, of being let down on deliveries; of quality not being up to samples submitted; of costly replacements; the sales offer must include confidence building sentences based on company analysis:

> 'Our company has been established only about twelve months, but our managing director was, for twenty years, chief engineer with the largest electronics firm in America. It is his vast experience that has developed our products.'

> 'We are only a small company, Mr Brown, but we are local. That means that you will get prompt and personal service, not only from me, but also from our managing director.'

> 'Because we are fairly small we operate only in a limited area. This keeps our costs down and we can pass the benefit on to you.'

The Larger Company

Sales managers and salesmen with a large organisation sometimes believe that the good reputation of their company ensures the confidence of its customers for ever. This might be true if there were no competitors, which is a rare occurrence.

A salesman working for a market leader should still evolve confidence building sentences, such as:

> 'We spend nearly three-quarters of a million a year on research, and you receive the benefit. Of course, the time will come when smaller companies will copy us, but by then we shall be even further ahead.'

> 'There is no special merit in being large, but we have grown so rapidly because we are efficient. We always strive to improve service for our customers, and we even give it at a loss, if necessary.' (The inference here is that a smaller company could not afford losses.)

> 'Because of our wide ramifications, Mr Brown, we can

offer you a free survey. Our electronics engineer will come
down here and evaluate.'

Every salesman criticises competitors' products indirectly,
and so every salesman must build confidence to refute the
implied criticism.

Although a customer may have dealt with a salesman for
many years, he must still be constantly reminded of the main
reasons for the company's high reputation.

Here are sentences which project the right image of a
company:

'May I arrange for you to visit our new factory? It is one
of the most up to date production units in the country, and
it would help you to impress upon *your* customers the value
they are buying.'

'Our company is sixty years old this month, but I know
you will agree that it is very young in its outlook, always
trying for better quality, better value.'

Whether a company is large or small, there is always some
aspect of its background which can be turned into a confidence
builder.

Even before analysing a product or service a salesman should
ask himself, *'Why should a buyer have confidence in my company?'*
Surely not because of a claim to be the longest established, or
the largest. Old established may be a euphemism for old
fashioned. One pictures a series of medals on a company's
headed notepaper—relics of exhibition awards in 1897—and,
then one thinks of obsolete plant, self-perpetuating directors,
and nepotism.

'We are the largest' can mean a newly acquired member of a
huge conglomerate, and conglomerates are only as good as the
management teams of their diversified companies.

To discover true customer benefits the salesman must use the
questioning technique, but the questions should be related not
only to a product but to the total ramifications of a company.
Every fact, every feature, must be analysed and the resulting
benefits incorporated in the sales offer. This is the reason for this
chapter being called *Offer* Analysis, and not Product Analysis.

Here are examples of the type of questions which could be asked:

What is special about our factory?

Do we use machinery that allows for better quality—finish—durability?

Do our management team have special qualifications? (e.g. our managing director is a technical adviser to a Government department; our research chemists have developed a substance of world-wide acclaim.)

Do localised depots help to speed deliveries?

In what way does our research and development team help our customers?

In what way do our exports help the home market?

How does the packing of our products help our customers?

How does our service department offer better service than our competitors?

The objective of offer analysis is to identify and list all product features, company advantages, advertising and promotional schemes and attributes of company personnel, and then turn these into benefits for the buyer.

Be Selective

A complete analysis may result in the listing of a hundred or more features leading to two hundred benefits. This is unusual, but it can happen, for example, when a salesman carries a wide range of component parts. However, in most cases the product analysis results in approximately ten features—twenty general benefits and, perhaps, thirty selective or personal benefits.

In many sales interviews a salesman can give his total sales offer, while at others he should be selective.

The complete analysis provides a salesman with a storehouse of features/benefits from which he can select those applicable to the buyer he is facing. The more thorough and complete his analysis, the better the salesman is able to select benefits which will motivate a buyer.

Another reason for the essential need of a complete analysis is to enable a salesman to evolve *double benefits*.

If the salesman is calling on an architect, consulting engineer, or any other specifying authority, the 'buyer' is concerned not only with the needs of his clients, but he also has to consider his own reputation and professional judgment. He has to be sure that he is giving the best advice, that standards will be maintained.

In the sales offer a salesman calling on a specifying authority would incorporate in his offer benefits to the 'buyer' *and* his client.

Beating Competition

Imagine now that you are selling a device used in the manufacture of a domestic appliance. This device, incorporating a special unit with a five-point control, allows the manufacturer to work to fine limits.

You decide that it is hardly worth while incorporating this feature in your sales offer because all three of your competitors, A, B, and C, also have five point controls on their devices. But the salesman of Company B does stress this well-known feature—and gets the order, the buyer being under the impression that B's device is different, having an additional advantage of a five point control, while others may only have a three or four unit control.

The buyer is only under this misapprehension because neither you nor the salesmen from A or C thought it worth while telling him about it.

Remember then, when working out your sales offer, not to leave out features/benefits which are taken for granted. Buyers are rarely as knowledgeable as they would like salesmen to believe. Always incorporate *standard benefits* in your offer, even if they can also be claimed by competitors.

Now you might ask this question:

'What happens when all competitors carefully work out their sales offers; when we all give similar benefits, who will get the orders?'

They will usually be placed with the salesman who has the ability to find that *extra* benefit.

Picture now a pair of jockey scales, with the buyer occupying the jockey's seat and you putting on the weights. The buyer is listening to your sales offer and considering whether he should buy from you, or not. These thoughts run through his mind:

> *Could I buy better elsewhere?*
>
> *Can I get a better price?*
>
> *Can I rely on what this salesman is promising?*
>
> *Will it break down?*
>
> *Will they be able to give immediate after-sales service?*
>
> *I don't think their locking device is as good as the one shown to me last week.*
>
> *I'd be safer to rely on Company B—I know them well.*
>
> *I'd better think it over.*

All the time he is weighing up your proposal, the weight of his negative thoughts depresses his side of the scale. The odds move against your getting an order. Then you begin to build strong benefits and gradually the scale tilts slightly in your favour. Eventually, to your great relief, as you add benefit upon benefit, your side moves sharply down; the buyer's moves upwards.

At the tenth benefit the scales are equally balanced. It is the moment of decision, but still the buyer hesitates and while he is undecided, you add one more benefit. It might be only of marginal importance—almost gossamer light in weight—'*The secondhand value keeps high, Mr Brown. In five years' time we can offer you . . .*' Your offer might be of small moment to the buyer, being only fractionally more than the figure suggested by a competitor, and insignificant compared with the total offer. To your delight you hear him saying, 'Perhaps it will do the job— the order is yours.'

The scale has been tilted only slightly, so slightly, in your favour—but it is enough.

We have been told by industrial salesmen that they have often remembered this story when the going was hard, and it reminded them *always* to look for that extra benefit to beat competition.

Now you may ask, 'But if I have worked conscientiously on the offer analysis, how can I possibly find an *extra* benefit?'

There is always one extra benefit, and the effort to find it is worthwhile.

Imagine your life depended on squeezing an orange dry with your hands. You are handed a medium-sized orange and told that if one drop of juice is left, your life will be forfeit. So you begin to squeeze, relax, squeeze again, relax, exert more pressure, and squeeze even harder. Finally, with aching hands and tired muscles you believe you have succeeded—you feel safe. Looking down at the inert, misshapen, dry mass of useless pulp you hear the voice of the executioner saying, 'It is not enough!' With fear adding to your strength you make a final determined effort. You squeeze; squeeze again. Nothing happens. You take a deep breath and exert every ounce of pressure. One more drop of juice drips slowly from the pulp.

Squeezing the orange has a message for all industrial salesmen. Your livelihood and an important order could depend on your ability to *squeeze* that extra benefit from the product. To do this you must think again of buying motivation—rational and emotional reasons why people buy, and you must check each feature again against each motivator. You may have overlooked the emotional appeal of pride, the rational appeal of security, or some tiny aspect in the history of your company which will give additional confidence to the buyer. You *must* find that extra benefit.

Telling Isn't Selling

Many industrial salesmen use words, sentences, expressions, and make statements which apparently offer benefits but which have no impact on the buyer. For example:

> *It will increase your profit.*
> *It will do a marvellous job.*
> *It is self cleaning.*
> *Everyone is delighted with the results.*
> *We can deliver them right away.*

Our service is first-class.

They are sold all over the world.

There are hundreds of these superlatives which sound fine to the salesman; but factual statements do not personalise a benefit, and it is personal benefits which motivate a buyer. Salesmen, therefore, need a constant reminder to explain benefits in terms of the buyers' interests.

You will never forget to personalise benefits if you will always remember these three link words:

which means that

They are sold all over the world is a confidence building sentence used by many salesmen; but by adding the words *which means that*, it can be considerably strengthened:

'They are sold all over the world, *which means that* your agents can get immediate service . . .'

We maintain huge stocks. What does that mean? How huge are the stocks? The word huge can be interpreted differently by different people. How much stronger when a salesman says:

'We maintain huge stocks *which means that* we can almost take over your inventory problems, and like others of our customers you will cut down on stocks by thirty per cent or more, because we deliver so quickly.'

By using the words *which means that* you will be certain to give the benefit YOU appeal. The YOU is, of course, the buyer. Every sale must have YOU appeal.

Here is an example of how a salesman can begin to work out his feature/benefit/YOU appeal for a specific type of fork lift truck:

features: Uses diesel oil or LP gas

benefits: 1. No need to recharge battery

2. No need for battery replacements

3. No depending on electrical means for recharging batteries

4. Gives maximum performance all the time.

These are all the facts derived from only *one* feature of the fork lift truck. There could, of course, be many more.

Now let us give these facts YOU appeal:

YOU Appeal: 1. No need for recharging batteries, which means that YOU will increase the work load without increasing costs. That is quite a saving.

2. No need for battery replacements, which means that YOU will cut costs and will not have the worry of breakdown through a battery fault.

3. YOU will not be dependent on electric mains for recharging the batteries, which means that your men will not have to waste time moving away to an electrical junction or running a cable. Your men can use the truck anywhere at any time—a huge advantage in a very busy factory like yours.

4. YOU will get maximum performance all the time, which means that the running costs are cheaper.

Here are other examples: Only *one* feature of the complete offer analysis is given:

Cellulose Wrapping Films

features: Ease of use.

benefits: 1. An inherently rigid film
                 2. Non-critical heatseal range
                 3. Non-burn-through of the film
                 4. Non static
                 5. Natural shrinkage.

YOU Appeal: 1. It will give you good machine ability and well-formed packs.

2. You will not require sophisticated temperature control equipment, nor a high level of maintenance.

3. You will not suffer rejections during production stops because of burn-through.

4. You will not experience static charge which could lead to complaints.

5. It will impart that extra film tightness to your product.

*   *   *

Centrifugal Pumps

features: Rotating element is in complete radial balance.

benefits: 1. Normal wear takes place symmetrically.

2. There is less wear on the pump bearings.

YOU Appeal: 1. You can get full hydraulic performance from the pump impeller for 75 % of its life.

2. You save money on maintenance, whereas normal centrifugal pumps would almost certainly require replacement of 'wearing' parts.

*   *   *

Control Relay

features: Add on auxiliary contact assemblies.

benefits: 1. Variety of contact arrangements.

2. Changes in operating sequences can be quickly accommodated.

3. Contact maintenance is simplified.

YOU Appeal: 1. Your requirements, however versatile, can be met simply by adding the appropriate contact block.

2. You have no need to change the relay. Simply change the add-on block.

3. Your maintenance staff can carry out maintenance on the bench rather than within the confines of the control panel.

*   *   *

Milling Machine

features: Automatic 'backlash' eliminator.

benefits: 1. Wear of leadscrew and nut minimised.

2. Climb milling is possible.

3. Better finish produced.

YOU Appeal: 1. You have less replacement costs.
2. You have higher production capability.
3. Your work is produced to higher standards.

* * *

Forms Handling Equipment
features: Electronic operation.
benefits: 1. Ease of operation.
2. Quickness of operation.
3. Simplicity of maintenance.
4. Cleanness of operation.
YOU Appeal: 1. You can easily train your staff.
2. You can have quicker running speeds.
3. You will have less downtime.
4 You have provided better working conditions.

* * *

Inert Gas System
features: Oxygen analyser.
benefits: 1. Ensures accurate O_2 measurement.
2. The only RINA approved unit.
3. Automatic cut off.
YOU Appeal: 1. Your gas is safe and reliable.
2. You are assured of acceptance by insurance companies.
3. Your system will close down if O_2 exceeds safe level.

To achieve the objectives of listing features/benefits/YOU appeal, and remembering *which means that*, a simple device can be used. *An Offer Analysis Sheet*. This sheet helps the salesman to organise his knowledge of his product or service in such a way that it becomes easy to link features to benefits, and then express these as personal benefits with the relevant YOU appeal.

As many sheets as necessary may be used. Fig A shows the design of an Offer Analysis sheet, and also shows how it is possible to derive from one feature three main benefits and seven YOU appeal benefits.

Figure B shows how to create features and benefits from back-up services. (In this example, product features have been excluded.)

Figure C is a complete analysis of a washer/extractor used for washing and drying very heavy loads in industry.

Figure D shows a complete analysis of a bucky table used in conjunction with X-ray equipment.

Figure A

OFFER ANALYSIS SHEET

Product or Service: Water Treatment

FEATURES Boiler Water Treatment	BENEFITS	'which means that' YOU APPEAL
	Prevents scale and corrosion in boiler.	The life of the boiler will be considerably lengthened, and reducing replacement time means cost reduction for you. You will reduce costs considerably because there will be no more tube replacement or scale removing by acid cleaning. Because of less down time you will get greater production.
	Prevents corrosion of steam return lines.	You will effect savings because the lines will have a much longer life.
	Improves oil combustibility.	You will be using fuel more efficiently, again reducing costs. Your insurance company will not load a policy relating to the boiler because you will have met their requirements.

Figure B

OFFER ANALYSIS SHEET

Product or Service: Industrial Perfumes

FEATURES	BENEFITS	'which means that'	YOU APPEAL
Market Research Division	Colour trends are monitored globally. The odour types likely to become popular are predicted. Tests are made in different marketing areas to confirm predictions.		The fragrance having been proven in the market place, you can be confident that your products contain a fragrance acceptable to the customer.
Environmental Research Division	Fully tests fragrance for all possible health hazards.		You will know that the fragrance is harmless. You will have no worry that the reputation of your company might be endangered by criticism from consumer groups.
Technical Service Division	Tests fragrance for physical stability and compatibility with product base.		Because fragrance has been fully tested prior to availability, all your questions relating to its uses can be answered instantly.

Figure B

OFFER ANALYSIS SHEET

Product or Service: Industrial Perfumes

FEATURES Product Study Group	BENEFITS 'which means that'	YOU APPEAL
	Monitors new product developments globally and assesses the possibilities of the product's expansion into new markets.	You will be kept up to date with new product trends, and you can offer compatible fragrances quickly.
	Ensures the development of an increasing number of suitable fragrances for different markets.	You will keep ahead of your competitors. You will hear of opportunities for expansion.

Figure C

OFFER ANALYSIS SHEET

Product or Service: Washer Extractor

FEATURES	BENEFITS 'which means that'	YOU APPEAL
Exclusive Floataire Suspension System	Isolates all vibration during hydro-extraction.	You can install the machine on any type of flooring, saving the expense of reinforcing.
	During washing, machine rests solidly on floor.	You obtain the essential firmness necessary for good washing action. You obtain maximum extraction efficiency.
	Cylinder is raised from floor during extraction process.	
	Automatic levelling of pneumatic mountings.	You are assured of an even load distribution.
Combination of Washing and Extraction in one machine	Eliminates need for separate extractor.	You double productivity and avoid unnecessary operation.
	Reduces standstill time.	You achieve greater output per operator per hour thus increasing efficiency.
	Fully automatic process.	You improve labour morale and increase efficiency
	Minimises wet floor	You improve working conditions and reduce the risk of accidents.

Figure C

OFFER ANALYSIS SHEET

Product or Service: Washer Extractor

FEATURES	BENEFITS	'which means that'	YOU APPEAL
Stainless Steel Cylinder	Non-corrosive.		There is less likelihood of staining. You will improve hygiene which is so vitally important.
	Easy to maintain in good condition.		Your maintenance costs will be low.
	More durable.		The stress on the cylinder structure in your machine is reduced when subjected to heavy loads.
	Special stainless steel welding preparation on cylinder ends.		
Automatic punched card	Controls complete process automatically from start to finish.		You eliminate manual control entirely saving on labour costs and reducing cycle time.
	Infinitely variable to suit any special process. Wash room operator utilised on other work during automatic process.		You save on water, steam and materials and generally reduce operating costs. You are prepared to adapt the control to process new synthetic materials or special M.O.H. requirements.
	Requires minimum attention other than periodical cleaning and adjustment.		You reduce your labour force and keep costs to a minimum. Your maintenance costs are low.
	Compact enough for mounting on main column of washer extractor.		There is space saving and it is easily accessible for your staff.

Figure C

OFFER ANALYSIS SHEET

Product or Service: Washer Extractor

FEATURES	BENEFITS	'which means that'	YOU APPEAL
Sliding loading doors	Permits rapid unloading and loading.		You reduce turn round time on the process.
	Ideally suited to chute loading system.		Increased automation means increasing your efficiency.
	Sliding arrangement on lined track for effortless loading and unloading.		You improve working conditions and reduce operator fatigue.
	Complete with hinged loading shelf.		You prevent the occurrence of articles falling between loading doors and the cylinder.
	Fully interlocked for safety.		You reduce the risk of accidents and provide a built-in safety regulation.

Figure C

OFFER ANALYSIS SHEET

Product or Service: Washer Extractor

FEATURES	BENEFITS 'which means that'	YOU APPEAL
Automatic Bearing Lubrication system	Proper level of oil metered into at appropriate intervals.	You increase efficiency of bearings by accurate lubrication. You will not need to spend time on periodical lubrication. You eliminate human error where bearings can be over or undercharged reducing life expectancy. You ensure the smooth running of the machine.

Figure D

OFFER ANALYSIS SHEET

Product or Service: Bucky Table (X-ray Equipment)

FEATURES	BENEFITS	'which means that'	YOU APPEAL
Unique floating and swivelling table top action	Very sick patient can be positioned quickly. Dispenses with need for moving heavy patients manually. Release of brake is operated by a foot pedal.		Your assistants' and nurses' time is saved. You and your assistants avoid physical strain or injury. You employ less effort and have one hand free for reassuring patient, etc.
The film is in the closest position to the table top	Magnification is reduced. There is less scattered radiation because of reduced film-patient distance. Avoids repeating films. Avoids having to use other specialised equipment, e.g. skull tables.		Your films are more nearly life-size. Your films are clearer and of better quality. Your time and film costs are saved. Your capital expenditure on equipment will be lower.

Figure D   OFFER ANALYSIS SHEET

Product or Service: _____   Bucky Table (X-ray Equipment)

FEATURES	BENEFITS 'which means that'	YOU APPEAL
The Bucky is in a fixed position	Movable X-ray tube is not necessary. Only one movement is required—that of bucky table.	You can utilise the smallest space possible. You will save time by not having to move (a) patient (b) tube (c) film.
Removable table top	Patient can be lifted directly from table to stretcher base, on the table top. Is easily cleaned and can be kept under sterile condition.	There is no risk of injury to the patient. You and your assistants are not likely to catch any infection or infect other patients from this source.
Solid, robust construction	Reliable. Very stable with heavy fixed base.	Is not likely to break down and you will not suffer inconvenience by having a table you cannot use. Your patient is not in any danger of falling as a table moves unexpectedly.
All table movements are mechanical	No electrical parts needed or a separate mains supply.	You save money on installation costs.

The ABC of Selling

While browsing in a book shop I became conscious of a conversation taking place between two people standing alongside me. I glanced around. He was obviously a salesman, she, I knew was the assistant buyer. Although the book titles mentioned are imaginary, the conversation went almost exactly like this:

'*Love Me Not* has been selling very well. How's it doing here?' asked the salesman.

'Not at all bad,' answered the assistant buyer.

'Oh, by the way,' said the salesman, a sudden thought obviously crossing his mind, 'You've been on holiday, haven't you?'

'Yes.'

'I hope you had a nice time.'

'It was a wonderful change.'

'Oh good! Shall we say six *Love Me Not*?'

'Yes, I think so. . . . Are you reprinting *How to Shoot Straight*?'

'I think we are—it's very good, isn't it?'

'It's been very popular.'

'I'll let you know about the reprint when I call next week.'

'There isn't any hurry, I think we still have one or two in stock.'

'No trouble—by the way, I notice you've taken *Birds and Their Feathers* off the table display.'

'We left it there for a week.'

'Fair enough! But it's going very well. By the way . . .'

What pathetic words—what lack of understanding on the part of the salesman.

'*Love Me Not* has been selling well, how is it doing here?' And what about the salesman's sudden switch to human rela-

tions—'By the way, you've been on holiday, haven't you?'
Surely that must have made you squirm as it did me. It was the
by the way that made it so ill-mannered. If he had said, 'Mrs
Harris, I'm so sorry—of course, you've been away. Where did
you go?' and had then listened carefully to the reply, it would
have been acceptable. But by sandwiching his remarks in
between a discussion about books it was so obviously an attempt
to win favour by showing some slight interest in her private life.

Now consider his answer to the inquiry about reprinting—'I
think so.'

If he was not sure of the position he should have answered,
'I'm so glad you asked that question. It's a book well worth
reprinting, isn't it? I'll telephone, and let you know before I
leave whether there is a reprint or not.'

These are positive words. But he revelled in his use of weak
words—by the way—I think—fair enough. . . .

It is more unusual to be able to listen to an industrial salesman selling, but before criticising the words of the publishers'
representative, every industrial salesman should ask himself the
question:

> *Does it apply to me? Do I use positive words, or do I rely on such
> words as maybe—could be—I think? When I string my words
> together do they result in weak sentences which lack appeal and
> persuasiveness?*

Almost every word a salesman uses should help him towards
his objective. Every sentence should condition the mind of the
buyer towards acceptance of his offer.

It has often been said that salesmen *live* by the words they use.
Is that true or false? Could a salesman succeed by remaining
silent during an interview, or by miming? Of course he couldn't!
If a salesman doesn't speak he cannot sell; and if he does speak,
he uses words. If he chooses the wrong set of words a sale is
much less likely than if he selects words which have meaning,
impact, even authority.

A salesman must have stamina, be able to fight back when that
big order is lost. He must strive for objectives in spite of continual government-inspired stop–goes. He should be sincere,

look presentable—but if he cannot select the right words to answer an objection or to stress a benefit of his products, he cannot succeed.

Consider the words given below (they are not 'opposites') and then decide that you will only use words and phrases which have the qualities listed in the left-hand column:

certain	casual
common-sense	careless
comprehensive	boastful
constructive	bitter
descriptive	doubtful
eager	empty
explicit	faltering
glowing	frivolous
good	futile
honest	flattering
impressive	blundering
clear	incoherent
significant	obsolete
potent	pathetic
stirring	pompous
direct	superfluous
strong	trite
understandable	incomprehensible
vivid	vague
appealing	angry
appropriate	nonsensical
creative	wondering
impressive	half-hearted
emphatic	pessimistic

A Logical Pattern

'I never forget a face,' says one man, then adds, 'but I can't remember names.'

Another will tell you that he always forgets birthdays, and a third will say ruefully that he sometimes can't even remember his own telephone number.

All of us, on occasion, have been asked by a stranger for directions to a street which we pass every day, but when the request is made we feel like foreigners in our own locality. We can't remember where the street is located.

There are many reasons given for a lapse of memory, but we are not concerned with the jargon of the psychologists explaining the temporary amnesia, or the platitudes of the schoolmaster—'Jones Minor, you are not taking any interest, that is why you cannot remember.' We have to concentrate only on the solution, and a solution must be found to enable the industrial salesman to remember every facet of his product or service and all the benefits derived from them.

Many a salesman has said to himself after leaving a buyer without an order, 'I forgot to tell him . . .', or, 'Why the hell didn't I tell him . . .' 'If only I had explained . . .'

While selling, we cannot consult a check list of features and benefits, and to succeed, we must remember all of the features/benefits at every call. Equally important, we must present them in a logical sequence, although there are occasions when the sequence should be changed. For example, when a product has several different applications, the main benefit for one buyer could be a subsidiary benefit for another.

As a salesman should always begin his offer with a main benefit rather than by stressing a minor point, a reversal of the usual order might be called for. For example, a salesman may be selling an industrial catering service. Perhaps his main feature is that his company will supply fully trained canteen staff. However, he may know in advance that a prospect is dissatisfied with the lack of menu variety supplied by a competitor. If the salesman is confident that his company can give the variety required it would be right for him to make this his main and first feature when he calls, rather than the supplying of trained staff.

It is usually unnecessary to alter the order of feature/benefits in a sales offer. If a salesman switches his appeal at almost every call he will, inevitably, forget some aspect of his product which might motivate a buyer to buy. It is important, therefore, that a salesman should arrange his benefits in a logical pattern, and all of us, on occasion, use a logical sequence in our private lives.

If we require a bank overdraft we do not, without thought, hurry to the bank, ask to see the manager, and immediately request a loan. Long before we are due to meet we have turned over and over in our minds exactly what we are going to say. We plant in our memory cells all the main reasons why we need a new car or an extension to the house, or extra stock for our business. Then we bring a pattern to these mind pictures, so that we have a story with a beginning, a middle, and an ending—a logical sequence. We even decide on the type of friendly greeting we shall use.

We build confidence by telling him how well we are doing. Then we extol the great advantages to us of having a car—how it will increase our business or protect our health. Or we explain the extra value which will be added to our property through an extension which we intend building. We conclude by telling him of the ease with which we can make repayments. Because we have rehearsed it in our mind so often we remember it, word for word. And the bank manager, whether he grants the loan or not, will hear the full story.

We do not say subsequently, 'I wish I'd told him . . .'

It is one of the important aids to a salesman's memory to be able to repeat his sales offer again and again in a similar pattern. There can be many interruptions and many variations during a sale, but if a product has twenty benefits, the salesman must present those twenty benefits to the buyer so that he is unlikely to forget any part of his sales offer, and must give them in a logical order.

It is natural for us to think in a logical order—that is the way our memory cells work. Here is an exercise to prove this point:

Answer quickly.

Give as rapidly as possible all the numbers between one and ten.

Automatically you repeated, *one two, three, four, five, six* . . .

You didn't mouth *eight, nine, seven, five, six* ... or begin at *ten* and work backwards. You thought of consecutive numbers because it was rational to do so. In the same way you will be able to remember all your features/benefits when you organise them from *one to ten, one to twenty*, or *one to thirty*, however many you may have.

The industrial salesman who wants to be sure that he will make the greatest impact at every call will

1. use positive words,
2. check the features and benefits on the offer analysis sheet;
3. use additional sheets to re-write these features/benefits, so that they form a logical pattern;
4. as an extra aid to memory, use *key sentences*.

Key Sentences

The Tack key sentence is a simple sentence related to a fact or feature of the product, which reminds the salesman of that fact or feature and the benefits related to it. As many sentences should be evolved as there are features/benefits.

Call back to your mind the first few words of the proverb, *Early to bed, early to rise*. Automatically into your mind flashes, *makes a man healthy, wealthy and wise*.

Once a key sentence is remembered it is almost impossible to stop the flow of words which build and elaborate on that sentence.

Here is another example: *A bird in hand* ... Could you stop yourself continuing with, *is worth two in the bush*? You almost certainly murmured these words to yourself, automatically.

Ask anyone over twenty to tell you the name of a well-known song from a very old musical show, *The Bing Boys*, staged about 1915. Few will be able to remember a song written so many years before they were born. But ask the same people to give you the next line from a song which begins: *If you were the only girl in the world* ... and seven out of ten will answer, *and I was the only boy*. These are the opening words of the song from that very, very old musical, *The Bing Boys*.

This is proof of how key sentences act as reminders, and

unlock the memory. It is a technique developed by Tack over the years, and is now used by salesmen all over the world as a memory aid.

Here are some key sentences: A salesman is selling a new external wall paint. The paint has a very important feature, eliminating the need for a lot of preparation work, including priming and sealing. An easily remembered key sentence could be:

You don't have to prime or seal.

This immediately highlights the obvious benefits of:

saving of time—important in factory maintenance

saving of labour—a very big benefit indeed where maintenance labour is scarce

saving of materials—a primer and a paint in one tin

a considerable saving on the hire of scaffolding.

With that single easily remembered sentence a salesman can pinpoint the YOU appeal so vital to his presentation.

A salesman offering catering services to industry could use this sentence:

Quality meals for your staff under your own roof.

These few words remind the salesman of the many factors which would show benefits to the buyer.

The *quality* of the meals which would ensure no complaints.

The *consistency* of the service.

The *efficiency* that backs it.

The dangers of staff having to go out midday, skipping meals, and therefore producing less work during the afternoon (own roof).

Staff who go out and arrive back late because of difficulty of getting a meal locally (own roof).

The effect on staff of seeing that management have the interests of their staff at heart (quality).

The retention of key personnel through this additional welfare (your staff).

Easier recruitment by offering extra facilities.

An excellent key sentence used by Dunlop is:

Dunlop Thixofix spreads like butter—grips like iron.

After voicing that sentence no salesman could fail to describe vividly the ease of application and the many uses of Thixofix.

The ABC of Selling

Remembering the product/benefit sequence, the industrial salesman will be able to present his case to the buyer in a logical, clear, and progressive manner, while averting the constrictions of a rigid sales formula.

He should also sell conversationally. The hallmark of the professional salesman is his ability to sell in a conversational manner, to relax the buyer while still maintaining his interest.

Conversational Selling

The majority of salesmen sound and act like salesmen. *And why not?* you may ask. *The buyer knows full well that I am a salesman, with the object of getting a decision from him.*

This is true, but we know that human behaviour does not change because a man has the authority of a decision maker. A buyer doesn't want to be continuously reminded that someone has set out to persuade him to do something which, five minutes earlier, he had no intention of doing. It needs to be stressed continually that buyers do not like taking risks. They prefer the *status quo*, the known, to the unknown.

A buyer wants to consider, to look again at a competitor's product, to ask the opinion of someone else, to delay matters. And the more he is conscious of a salesman urging him to make up his mind, the more he will resist coming to a decision.

Selling jargon always switches on the red warning light in a buyer's mind. Phoney persuasiveness scares him, crude, tough tactics annoy him, lack of common sense can infuriate him, and fast talking worries him. But when a buyer is involved in a conversation—a friendly conversation—he is apt to forget that a sale is taking place that someone is trying to persuade him to do something, to influence his mind.

Conversational selling is natural persuasion, but it is not easy to master. The simplest way is to learn to relax, because a relaxed salesman always sells conversationally which, in itself,

relaxes a buyer. A tense salesman invariably tenses a buyer—
and a tense buyer rarely buys.

A conscious effort must be made by all salesmen to sell conversationally; even if it is not possible to relax, a salesman must
make a great effort to sell in the same way as he would discuss
his problems with his family or his friends—in a natural manner.

Steps to the Order

Over the years, many a sales formula has been developed to
enable a salesman to be logical in his presentation. The basic
idea behind every standard sequence was that they would
concentrate the salesman's mind on the selling fundamentals so
that he could present his case in a logical and orderly manner.
But helpful as they were, they were not the complete answer to
a salesman's problem, which is to remind himself of the steps he
must cover if he is to give a complete sales offer.

Let us consider some of the *steps to the order* which have been
used over the past twenty years:

> attention
> interest
> desire
> action

How can *attention* be separated from *interest*? It is only possible
to hold a buyer's attention by creating immediate interest. So
these two steps must be combined.

Logically there can be no reason for a separate step *creating
desire*. *Desire* (*want* is a more appropriate word) must be created
from the opening of the sale to the close. There cannot be only
one step devoted to persuading the buyer to *want* a product or
service.

Here is another example:

> approach
> creating interest
> creating confidence
> selling the product benefits
> creating desire
> close

In this sequence *creation of confidence* is shown as an additional step. This is, undoubtedly, a move in the right direction, because it reminds a salesman of the essential need, whether he is well-known or unknown to a buyer, whether he has been calling on a company for years or weeks, to maintain confidence always.

It is right, therefore, for all salesmen to create confidence quickly but if a salesman leaves it at that he may still not eliminate the buyer's concern (new suppliers may have let him down in the past).

Creating confidence cannot be a single step, it must be established and re-established throughout the sale.

Here is another example:

    introduction
    finding needs
    benefits
    investment
    close

It is surely wrong to label the opening remarks of a salesman as an *introduction*. It is true he is introducing his sales offer to the buyer, but no one is introducing him to the buyer. The word *introduction* itself seems to be a relic of the last century, when salesmen wore top hats.

Finding needs is an essential step in selling, but whenever possible, a salesman should discover the *needs* before the call is made. This is a part of sales planning. If a buyer's needs are unknown, a salesman cannot ask the direct question, 'What are your needs?' The true need may take a long time to establish.

Investment, on the face of it, is a good step. It is right to prove to a buyer that he is not only buying to fill an immediate need, but that he is also making a safe investment for the future. But this is a benefit that might have to be established quite early in the sales offer. There is no reason why, suddenly, towards the end of a sale, the salesman should explain the benefit of investment.

Here is another example:
    attention
    interest
    conviction
    action

Every salesman should offer proof to substantiate the claims he is making. Sales points can be proved by the use of testimonial letters, letters of reference, copies of a paper written by an authority on the subject, articles in trade journals, research reports and Government reports. But the offering of such proof is not a separate step. Every benefit given must carry *conviction*, and proof should be given to a buyer point by point.

After many years of teaching and research we know that separate steps to remind the salesman to *create confidence*, to *emphasise benefits*, to *summarise*, to *create interest*, no longer apply. Nor is there a need for a separate step for a salesman to *answer objections*.

For all that, every attempt to find the ideal sequence has been helpful to salesmen. From the days of scripts to be learned and spoken parrotwise by salesmen, many ideas have been evolved and tried with varying success. Most of them failed to be the complete answer because they were too rigid, too impersonal, too unnatural, or difficult to remember; but for all that a salesman must have guide lines if his presentation is not to lack impact.

The Tack Organisation have always believed that selling should be made easy rather than difficult, and we are always researching to this end. The ideal is for a salesman to use his personality to good effect, which is not possible if restrictions are placed on him. For a salesman to be told exactly what he has to say is strait-jacketing his mind.

Tack believe that although a sales manager may provide his salesmen with guide lines, he should not attempt to put a set of words into their mouths. A salesman must evolve his *own* sentences, his *own* manner of elaborating benefits derived from features.

We know that a salesman should sell conversationally. We

know that by repetition he will present his benefits in a logical order. We know that by memorising key sentences he will be able to elaborate each benefit, giving the maximum YOU appeal.

The object of the *opening* is to secure the undivided *attention* of the buyer. The object of the *close* is to obtain a decision.

Sandwiched in between are all the *benefits*. And to ensure that not a single feature is omitted, nor a benefit forgotten, all benefits should be presented in a logical sequence.

It's as simple as ABC—

*A*ttention

*B*enefits

*C*lose

These are the only steps a salesman has to remember, to enable him to succeed in selling.

The Opening . . .
Getting the Attention of the Buyer

The hand of the speedometer wavers around ninety miles an hour. Automatically he glances at the rear mirror to check whether or not a police car is trailing him; silently he curses the howling, crackling, useless car radio. The agony of not knowing is unbearable, but if he can average seventy he may still make home in time to see the last hour's play in the test on television . . . eighty runs needed, four wickets to fall . . .

With screaming brakes the car almost bucks to a halt. He leaps out, races up the garden path and digs his fingers again and again in the bell push. 'Come on, come on!' he urges, regretting now more than ever the loss of his front door key.

His wife eventually opens up. Pecking at her cheek and just missing, he is about to hurry to the TV room when he hears her say, 'You've got to do something about your mother. She was on the 'phone three times again today complaining.'

He mumbles comforting words as he edges his way to the television set. She trails alongside him, rat-tat-tatting on about her problem with her mother-in-law.

Suddenly he realises the enormity of his problem. If he switches on the television he will be ticked off for lack of interest in his wife's troubles, and she will sulk all night. If he doesn't switch on he may miss a fall of a wicket. He decides to use one of his standard ploys. Holding his head in his hand he murmurs, 'It's been a helluva day, and I've got a stinking head—I can hardly hold it up.'

Immediately, his wife breaks off her monologue saying sympathetically, 'I'll get you some aspirin and a cup of tea.'

No sooner does she leave the room than he switches on the

television and flops into his chair. When she returns, he interrupts her renewed diatribe about his mother with a periodic, 'Oh dear!' or, 'I am sorry!'

Later his wife says, 'So what are you going to do?'

'About what?'

'Your mother.'

'What about mother?' And that, of course, starts the row to end all rows, which need never have happened.

The mistake the wife made was in not finding the appropriate moment to raise her mother-in-law problem. She tried to influence him to take a line of action when his mind was concentrating on something else. She was selling under adverse conditions, and if the conditions are wrong we can rarely persuade anyone to do anything.

Self-Made Adverse Conditions

A salesman can create adverse conditions for himself during the first few seconds of an interview:

1. By *looking hopelessly around the buyer's office for somewhere to park his soaking wet coat or umbrella*. A salesman should always leave his coat/umbrella outside the buyer's office, whenever possible.

2. By *slamming the door behind him*. A slammed door can cause intense annoyance to a buyer.

3. By *gabbling*. When a salesman speaks too quickly or slurs his opening words, a buyer will not strain to hear what is being said. His attention will wander, and he may cut the interview short.

Many salesmen let their words pour out when they meet a buyer for the first time, or when hoping to close a big order. This is due to nervousness from which even the most experienced of salesmen is not immune.

He should not enunciate every word as if the buyer were a moron, but neither should he gabble. He need only speak a little more slowly than usual.

4. By *using weak or insulting sentences*. 'Insults,' you may exclaim, 'nonsense! No salesman begins by insulting a buyer.' To this reasonable assumption he should add the word *knowingly*.

Here are some examples of insulting openings:

'I was just passing by and thought you would want to see me about . . .'

'I thought I'd just pop in to ask if . . .'

To a buyer these remarks imply that his business, in the view of the salesman, does not warrant a special call. Also, this type of sentence undermines the self-importance of the buyer.

Neither should a salesman use a semi-apologetic opening:

'If I'm not troubling you too much . . .'

'I wonder if you would mind . . .'

'Forgive me if I'm intruding on your time, but . . .'

Weak openings only diminish the salesman in the mind of the buyer.

Never make adverse conditions for yourself.

BUYER-GENERATED ADVERSE CONDITIONS

A *buyer-generated adverse condition* is any situation in which a salesman, *through no fault of his own*, finds it impossible to obtain the undivided attention of the buyer.

Here are examples—problems and solutions which have been provided by delegates at our Selling to Industry Course.

Selling on the Shop Floor

The reason for your visit is to finalise an order. You have an appointment to see works director, John Brown. You arrive five minutes before the appointed time to be told by the receptionist that Mr Brown is in A Shop. As you are well-known to her she suggests that it would save time, as you have an appointment, if you went upstairs and waited for Mr Brown outside his office. There you meet his secretary, who tells you that her chief will be at least another thirty minutes, and adds, 'Would you rather make another appointment? Or if you care to, you can go down to A Shop.'

You decide to visit the factory floor. On arrival at A Shop you see Mr Brown in conversation with three machine operators. Approaching them and realising that they are having a heated argument, you back away and ask a fitter standing near by if there is a crisis.

He tells you that there is trouble because a machine has broken down. Pending repairs the shop foreman wants the machine operators to do other work and this, backed by their shop steward, they refuse to do, claiming that it might put a production bonus at risk. Mr Brown is trying to sort things out ...

Mr Brown sees you and calls out, 'I won't be a few minutes and I'll be with you.'

*   *   *

What do you do?

A. Wait for Mr Brown to be free?
B. Return to his office and wait for him there?
C. Make an appointment for another occasion?

The decision of the delegate was to return to Mr Brown's office and leave a short note for him. He wrote:

> *I appreciate your willingness to keep the appointment, but realise you have to give priority to the problems on the shop floor. I thought, therefore, you would prefer me to call again and see you later in the week. Miss Howell* (Mr Brown's secretary) *has suggested that Friday at 11 a.m. may be convenient for you, and I shall telephone her this afternoon to confirm that this is so.*

The delegate believed that if he had attempted to finalise details of the new installation on the shop floor he would have failed. He also believed that even if Mr Brown had accompanied him to his office, the buyer would still have been thinking about whether or not he had settled the problem in A Shop.

The delegate said he will never know whether or not he would have got the order if he had stayed, but that he *did* get it when he called on the following Friday.

Selling in the Factory Canteen

The competition has been intense, but you are confident that you have won a very large order for paper shredders. When you call on Bill Roberts, the managing director, for final approval, he keeps you waiting for some time then apologises, and invites you to have lunch with him. 'Over lunch,' he says, 'you can answer the few remaining questions still in my mind.'

Roberts, in his early thirties, is a self-made entrepreneur, a strong-minded, determined, but very friendly person. You have met him twice previously, and although he made it clear on each occasion that he was not prepared to have his time wasted and that he wanted direct answers to direct questions, you felt that you had impressed him.

Instead of taking you to a private restaurant, he conducts you to the staff canteen on the top floor. In one corner of the canteen-cum-restaurant the tables are occupied by the company executives. Reading your mind he says, 'We're all workers here—I don't believe in executives eating in lavishly decorated rooms. Actually, it's very good of our staff to allow us to eat with them.'

You laugh dutifully. He guides you to a table with seating for eight. Six of the seats are already occupied. After shaking hands with the six men, three of whom you have already met, you are led to the self-service counter to collect your meal.

Soon after returning to the table the bantering begins. They rib each other, and then gently pull your leg about the ethics of salesmen.

After a while Roberts says, 'I want you to tell me again why you think your shredders are better than those made by X, which cost fifteen per cent less.'

One of the executives says, 'They both shred papers. Five per cent I could understand, but how can you possibly justify fifteen per cent more?'

* * *

Do you immediately answer the question raised by the executive?

Do you again sell Roberts and all his colleagues on the benefits of your shredders?

Do you talk to the table in general?

Do you concentrate on the executive who emphasised the difference in cost of the two machines?

Or, Do you make an attempt to get away from the group?

The course delegate told us that he knew that if he became involved in a cut and thrust discussion with the executives they would do their best to pull his story to pieces, if only to prove to Bill Roberts what keen minds they had.

He said to the managing director, 'Mr Roberts, it would not be helpful to you or your colleagues if I were to detail the value and benefits of our shredders to you now. I left my case in your office and in that case is back-up evidence to justify your buying our *quality* shredder. Without that evidence you could come to the wrong decision, and that would be unfair to you. When I called previously, Mr Roberts, you insisted that you only wanted to hear facts. I promise you that when we return to your office I can give you all the facts required to prove that we can offer you the best value on the market.'

To the delegate's delight Mr Roberts said, 'I agree,' and then switched the conversation, and other matters were discussed. On returning to the managing director's office, the order was signed.

Never in the Corridor

You call to see a financial director, Douglas Hardy, to progress the sale of a new type of accounting machine in which Hardy is interested. He is a difficult man to sell to because on each occasion you have seen him he has thought of new applications for the machine.

On your way to his office you meet him in a corridor and he says, 'You're the very man I want to see. I'm concerned about the input . . .'

* * *

Do you listen to his query and deal with it on the spot?

Do you suggest that it is very difficult to show him the necessary drawings while standing in the corridor, and that it would be better if you both went to his office?

The delegate told us that he took the first course and dealt with the problem. Hardy then raised another point. The discussion lasted some fifteen minutes, after which Hardy made an excuse, shook hands with the delegate, and walked quickly away.

Eventually, the order went to a competitor.

He believed that one of the reasons he lost the sale was because he was at a distinct disadvantage while selling in the corridor. The interview had been cut short just when he was about to press home some of the strongest benefits of his machine. If they had been in Hardy's office the delegate would not have been summarily dismissed and could have found out Hardy's real objection to placing the order.

Buyers often make a point of seeing a salesman in a waiting-room, entrance hall, or corridor, because they know that they can always walk away. This is the most common of all *buyer-generated adverse conditions*.

There are many other examples of adverse conditions—when a buyer is about to leave for home; when the canteen manager is extremely busy, between twelve noon and two p.m.; when the warehouse manager is involved with an awkward delivery problem.

If you consider the conditions for selling are adverse it is better not to begin to sell,

BUT

it isn't always easy to decide whether or not the conditions are adverse. A salesman must not always believe a buyer who says, 'I'm very busy,' or 'I can only spare five minutes,' or 'I have another appointment shortly.' The buyer may just be seeking an excuse to get rid of a salesman *before* he has heard the salesman's proposition. Buyers delight in creating adverse conditions, but they can be overcome by a salesman's ability to sell well and to create immediate interest in his offer.

When in doubt, stay put. When you know that the odds are really against your being able to explain your proposition, or that it is impossible to hold the buyer's attention because of his *real* preoccupation with other matters, then leave him and try again another day.

THE FIRST CALL

All salesmen have to make first time calls at some time or another, but whether a salesman meets a buyer for the first time or the one hundredth time, he still has to gain and hold the buyer's attention during the first few minutes of the interview. On most occasions a busy buyer wants a salesman to explain quickly the purpose of his visit, but there is a friendly type of buyer who doesn't mind a few pleasantries before hearing the salesman's offer. These pleasantries, whether lasting seconds or minutes, can be called the *chat gap*.

Sometimes a courteous and friendly buyer, when first meeting a salesman, will offer him a seat and make some relaxing comment—for example, 'What a day! Did you get very wet walking from our car park? It's too far away from the factory block.'

This is an invitation for the salesman to reassure the buyer, in the fewest possible words, that all is well and he did not get really wet because he had an umbrella/mac, which he left in the waiting-room/hall/corridor. But the buyer's friendly greeting is not an invitation for the salesman to relate what happened once when he called at a factory whose car park was even farther away from the factory block.

At a first call, except when a buyer indulges in a few pleasant words, the salesman should determine to gain the buyer's undivided attention with his opening sentence. The *chat gap*, however, may lengthen when the salesman calls back regularly on the buyer.

Over the years a friendship may develop which would make it ridiculous for the salesman to attempt to grip the buyer's immediate attention. The buyer may have been ill, away on holiday, or at a conference. He may have been honoured in some way, or his wife may have had a baby. It is then only natural for the salesman to begin by saying, 'Are you quite well again now?' or, 'Was it a boy?' or, 'You were very good on TV last Wednesday.'

There is nothing wrong with such friendly remarks, but again, the salesman's objective is to keep them short. By keeping to one simple rule a salesman can always be sure of reducing the length of the *chat gap*. The rule is:

> *Never, never talk about yourself—your interests—your hobbies— your holidays—your family—your car—your accident or your health. Never give your opinion uninvited on the political situation, the election, or world affairs.*

If you do, the *chat gap* will lengthen and you will, inevitably, bore the buyer. Even if the buyer asks you about yourself out of politeness—your hobbies, children, etc.,—answer in as few words as possible. 'They're fine thank you' is quite enough. He doesn't really want to hear more, he is only being polite.

If a salesman is foolish enough to talk about himself he can be certain of one fact: The buyer won't listen and will, possibly, cut short the interview saying, 'I'm so sorry but I have to leave you, I have another appointment.'

Because it is so difficult for anybody to believe that lessons in human relations apply to them, many salesmen will say, 'But in my case it is different—my buyers like to hear about my . . .'

They do not.

GETTING ATTENTION

Whether the *chat gap* lasts five seconds or five minutes, as soon as it ends it is vital for the salesman to gain the buyer's attention by interesting him in the opening of his sales offer. There are five proven techniques, each of which can enable a salesman to get the buyer's attention time and time again. These techniques can be used at the first call or at the tenth call.

Here they are:

the factual opening
the question opening
the reference opening
the sales aid opening
the demonstration opening.

And for those who call back regularly on their clients, there is an additional technique which can be used:

the link opening.

Factual Opening

All of us have an insatiable desire to learn facts about subjects which interest us. What other reason is there for the Guinness Book of Records being a world best seller? If we are sending our son to a new school, all the facts we can gather about that school are read avidly. If someone is considering emigrating, he will read every fact he can about the country in which he hopes, eventually, to live. Just think of the brochures we study when we are planning a holiday abroad. We lap up the facts—six miles of sand, a hundred and fifty-two restaurants, eight golf courses, four swimming pools ...

Why should a buyer be any different in his thinking? We know he is no different, that he is motivated in the same way as we all are. A buyer's attention can always be held by a fact, or a series of facts, if they are directly connected with his business; and his attention is just as likely to be held on the fiftieth call by a fact which concerns his business as he was by one which interested him on the first call.

Here are some examples of factual openings:

'Mr Brown, it is a fact that oil fuels contain more energy in a given volume than any other fuel, but not all fuels are consistent and dependable. With X we guarantee ...'

'Very few companies need a huge hardware investment. It is a fact that most businesses only need day to day assistance for productive work in factory or office. Our new ...'

'There is now a way of fixing very heavy objects to a cavity wall without having to use special plugs or studding ...'

'Mr Smith, in a recent report from the World Health Council it was stated that noise was a main cause of stress in business. Our triple glazing will ...'

'Mr Williams, you can now have up to 1,500 internal

telephone extensions. As your plant covers so many acres I am sure you will be interested in our new . . .'

'As you know, Mr Johnson, it is an unfortunate fact that vandals are continually breaking factory windows on this estate. It need not happen to your factory any more, because we have a new glass . . .'

'It is not generally known, Mr Jennings, but one electric convection oven can cook eight hundred meals in eight minutes.'

The Question Opening

Ask a silly question and you'll get a silly answer, is an old tag, but conversely, and equally true, is: Ask a sensible or serious question and you will always get a sensible answer.

Only those facing hostile interrogation refuse to answer questions. The rest of us do so with pleasure, either instantly, or after some thought.

When we are in a furniture shop and the assistant says, 'What is the present colour scheme in your bedroom?' we are eager to tell him the design of our curtains, the colouring of the carpet, and the matching tones of the upholstery and the wallpaper.

One simple question involves us immediately in his sales offer.

If the car salesman asks us, 'Will you be using the car abroad as well as in this country?' we can hardly wait to tell him of our projected tour across the Continent.

Buyers always react to a question by becoming involved in the sale. Whether you have to influence the mind of a purchasing manager, personnel officer, shop foreman, design engineer or project engineer—if you ask him a question you will immediately obtain his undivided attention. Don't be concerned, however, at the brevity of his reply. He is involved in the sale. He might answer at length, but even if he only says, 'Yes' or 'No', it still allows you to elaborate, and you will have achieved your objective.

Here are some examples:

'Mr Smith, is it right that from this factory you export to nearly every part of the world?'

'Yes, we're very proud of our exporting achievements.'

'Then you will be interested to hear of our new daily world wide cargo flights.'

* * *

'Mr Kendal, am I right in saying that it is essential for you to use refrigerated vans for delivery?'

'Yes.'

'Then you will be interested in our ...'

* * *

'Mr Laurie, I am sure you will agree that everyone, these days, should consider ways of reducing pollution.'

'Yes, I certainly agree with that.'

'Well we have designed a revolutionary exhaust system to eliminate completely those intensely choking diesel fumes. Our new ...'

* * *

'Mr Brown, is it right that one of your main problems is the risk of water getting into the bearings?'

'That's a problem we always have.'

'Well Mr Brown, our new plastic covered bearings can relieve you of that worry, because ...'

* * *

'Mr King, can your present photocopier copy right up to the spine of a ledger?'

'No.'

'But you do think it would be helpful to you if it did?'

'Yes, on occasion perhaps.'

'Well our new Fotoit will.'

* * *

'Mr Staples, do you agree that dynamic expanding businesses like yours need up-to-the-minute information at very short notice?'

'Of course, it is essential.'

'Well Mr Staples, providing up-to-the-minute systems is our business.'

* * *

There is, of course, a similarity between stating a fact and asking a question. A fact can be turned into a question, in the same way as many questions can be changed into facts. But there is one difference in these openings: With the Question Opening the salesman expects, and gets, a reply. With the Factual Opening he states the fact, arouses the buyer's interest, but does not pause for an answer. He continues with his sales offer.

The Reference Opening

What is the ideal attention-getting technique? If used properly, it is the Reference Opening.

Let us think again of what immediately interests us. When considering a holiday in some sun-baked Mediterranean resort, we cannot make up our minds which of the hotels in the packaged deal to choose; and then a friend says to us, 'You must stay at the Capitol Hotel, it's absolutely marvellous. The food is wonderful and the service can't be bettered. Do you know they even . . .'

Do we hesitate? Not for a moment! We book up at the Capitol and tell everyone we meet that we are staying at a highly recommended hotel.

We need dental treatment and a friend says, 'You should go to Mr Williams in the High Street. He is the most marvellous dentist I've ever known. He hates giving you pain. You know how nervous I am generally.'

Off we go to meet Mr Williams.

And what do we do when a business acquaintance says, 'Why don't you go and see Mr Lane of Kerr Brothers about this? It seems just right for him. He's a friend of mine—mention my name.'

We very quickly telephone Mr Lane for an appointment, and

Mr Lane will, undoubtedly, see us, because he knows his friend wouldn't waste his time.

The mind of the buyer is always influenced by a recommendation from someone he knows. It can also be influenced if he is shown, very early in the interview, a letter stressing the benefits of your products, written by an executive of a company of repute.

But never use a letter written by a buyer's competitor. That could antagonise him.

Also, be careful about showing a letter from a giant organisation to the managing director employing some fifty people. His response could be, 'It's all right for them with their millions, but we are not big enough.'

The Sales Aid Opening

Scene I. Father is in the kitchen studying the football results. Mother enters, accompanied by daughter. The daughter places on the table a large irregularly shaped parcel. Father glances at it, then returns to the pools. He glances again. No one says anything. Eventually, even the report on a key match involving his home team cannot hold him. 'What's in that?' he demands, pointing at the parcel.

* * *

Scene II. The managing director is reading through important documents. His secretary enters and places a registered envelope on his desk. The managing director doesn't even pretend he is not interested.

Turning away from the important documents he asks, 'What's in that?'

* * *

What is it that makes husbands put down newspapers, and tycoons turn away from important matters?

Curiosity!

When a buyer sees a salesman unwrapping a small parcel, or opening a case in which something gleams brightly, or taking a plastic container from his pocket, that buyer will not want the salesman to leave before he has found out what it is that is gleaming in the leather case—what new concept is in the plastic container—what is so special about that parcel.

The Sales Aid Opening being based on the natural curiosity of most people will always get a buyer's undivided attention.

When the buyer sees a salesman take from his case a well-designed leaflet or an appealing brochure, curiosity and interest are aroused. When he is handed a piece of material he is curious to discover its benefits for himself. If he is purchasing industrial perfumes for use in a new product, his sense of smell will quickly involve him in the sales offer. A salesman selling foodstuffs to an industrial canteen manager will find that tasting allows the buyer to sell himself on the flavour, and a buyer will strain to hear if a salesman shows apparatus claimed to be almost silent in operation.

If, by using a sales aid, you can cover all of the prospect's five senses—sight, touch, taste, smell, and hearing—you will make a very good opening. This can rarely be achieved, but the objective should be to appeal to as many of the senses as possible.

Catalogues, descriptions, or specifications of equipment, photographs of installations, independent test reports, performance graphs, reproductions of testimonial letters from well-known companies, all can be used as a Sales Aid Opening.

Also used currently by salesmen at the opening are:

A sample 6 in. square showing the formation of the joint of the tongue and groove flooring chipboard.

Example of use of paper, e.g. airline tickets.

Photograph of new canteen equipment on location.

Small length of hose and coupling to show construction and quality.

Sample of special weld blending.

Fabrics.

All types of components.

Mouldings.

You do not want the buyer, at the opening, to read through a brochure line by line. He would only pretend to do so, anyway.

When using literature as a Sales Aid Opening, the salesman must pinpoint one particular feature applicable to the buyer's business. The salesman should always maintain control of the interview by holding the leaflet and pointing out the features. He should not hand it over for the buyer to study, enabling him to glance casually at each page, with a half-hearted interest which could lead him to decide that he is not interested.

The Sales Aid Opening can be most effective if linked with a Factual, or Question Opening.

The Demonstration Opening

Pen and paper can provide an excellent Demonstration Opening, which can immediately involve a buyer in the sales offer.

A salesman's opening sentence could be:

'We can move ten of your crates in ten minutes. Overall, this will mean a saving in time of . . .'

The salesman then writes down the total number of crates handled in a week and begins working out the overall saving in time. And from then on to cost reduction (continually involving the buyer in the calculations).

If, however, you are able to demonstrate equipment, the buyer will be quickly involved so there is very little need for attention-getting sentences.

Here are examples currently used by salesmen:

Cut-away model of electronic solenoid control valves.

Booster amplifiers to simulate operation.

Scale-model motorised sweeper.

Working model of ultrasonic level control.

Single booth tape recorder for buyer to test quality and versatility (language laboratory).

Internal bathroom/toilet air extractor unit with timing device.

'Lego' for demonstrating a layout of warehouses, showing racking systems, etc.

Small scale working model of generator plant, to show different areas that could need monitoring.

When demonstrating at the opening of a sale, remember these points:

1. Never demonstrate with an imperfect unit.
2. Whenever possible, let the buyer sell himself on the unit by allowing him to work the model.
3. Demonstrate very slowly. Make sure that your prospect is following each point, by asking him questions.

Sometimes it is better to list features/benefits of a unit before the demonstration takes place. On other occasions, however, a Demonstration Opening can be most effective, with each benefit being stressed as the demonstration progresses.

CALLING BACK

There are many reasons for industrial salesmen calling back on prospective buyers or customers, but whatever the objective, they can all be termed *Development Calls*. At every contact, high or low, a salesman attempts to develop the worth and profitability of the relationship.

Here are some examples:

To negotiate long-term business.

To get products or services specified.

To get repeat orders.

To close orders after days, weeks, months of negotiation.

To carry out a survey.

To see those who can influence decisions.

To try once more to open an account.

To introduce new units in a range.

To handle a complaint.

To discover the real reason why a competitor is obtaining business (buyers rarely give the real reason for changing).

To maintain goodwill by showing operators how to get the best out of equipment sold.

To get an introduction to another buyer.

To make certain when taking over a new territory that customers know all the benefits of products and the full range of company's services.

To gain knowledge of production conditions.

To get agreement to visit a factory or stage a demonstration of equipment.

To establish further needs with design department.

To get agreement from the production manager to allow a visit to his works by a prospective buyer.

To present quotation, specification, costings, changes in schedule.

Let us consider three of these objectives, and how they can be tackled by salesmen:

1. *To maintain goodwill and keep out competition by showing machine operators (or any other employees) how to get the best out of the equipment.*

Does the salesman approach the machine operators (having first, of course, obtained permission) and say, 'I know you're all a bit thick, so I thought I'd call to show you how to obtain the best results from the equipment', or, 'It hardly seems possible, but even now some of you don't know the full capabilities of the equipment!'

You can imagine the results if a salesman were to use these openings. He, therefore, has to take great care to plan in advance what he is going to say, so ensuring that there is no risk of antagonising anyone. His objective is to make sure that all the operators are well sold on the equipment, so that when new orders are placed they will speak highly of the equipment.

The salesman could use any of the standard openings—asking a question or stating a fact:

'Do any of you find difficulty in using the threaded . . .?'

'I have found on some calls that operators have not been told initially that by using the barlock at No. 10 frequency there is no risk of . . .'

In neither of these openings does he risk upsetting the operators, and he is using exactly the same *form* of opening as he would use if his object was to sell the equipment, instead of calling back to maintain goodwill and increase product knowledge.

2. *To get an introduction to another buyer.*

In exactly the same way as if he were selling, the salesman

would plan how to phrase the opening sentence. He might ask a question:

> 'Mr Brown, do you know if Mr Kenton in your S Division uses block struts as you do here?'
>
> 'I'm not certain.'
>
> 'Then would you mind introducing me to him so that I can see if we can be as helpful to his division as we always try to be to yours?'

3. *To discover the real reason why a competitor is obtaining business* (buyers rarely give the real reason).

To achieve this objective can be difficult. Would it be achieved by trying to wheedle the information out of an employee? Surely this form of ferreting out information borders on the unethical. The salesman might, therefore, decide to use a Fact-plus-Question Opening when talking to a friendly employee:

> 'John, as you know we supply over sixty per cent of the Cyclatones in the British Isles and that percentage increases every year. But we still don't want to lose any of it. Can you tell me, therefore, if there is any reason why Mr Johnson, your buyer, has decided to use Cyclatones supplied by XYZ?'

Most people will react to a direct question, and John will probably be no different from others.

Although the objectives of a salesman may be varied and may cover a wide area, the majority call to negotiate or obtain orders.

Sometimes a salesman can call on a buyer twenty times or more, attempting to open the account. Salesmen supplying customers with component parts may call every four weeks on a buyer; others may call two or three times a year,

BUT

following the *chat gap*, a salesman must still obtain the undivided attention of the buyer—assistant buyer—research and development manager—accountant—or whoever it is whose mind the salesman has to influence.

Every salesman, at every call then, must have an objective,

and on that objective will be based the opening technique he will use. Without an objective a salesman risks using a colourless, cliché-ridden opening, which makes it so easy for a buyer to end the interview quickly.

Here are examples of weak call-back openings:

'Any news for me?'

'Have you heard from the Board yet?'

'Have you had a chance yet of discussing the matter with the contractors?'

'I hope you have some good news for me today.'

'Have you arrived at a decision yet?'

'Were you able to check the stock?'

Following this type of weak opening it is so easy for a buyer to reply negatively: 'No, the Board hasn't yet decided'; 'No, I haven't studied the quotation yet'; 'No, I haven't had the stock checked since you last called; come back again in four weeks' time.'

As much care must be taken with a Call-Back Opening as with a first call. All of the standard techniques can be used when calling back.

Here are examples:

Factual Opening:

'Because of the world shortage of Salycotes we shall shortly be changing to a synthetic I felt sure you would want to place a large order now, while the Salycotes are still available.'

Factual Opening:

'Mr Smith, you are using approximately 120,000 metres of Dylet a month. An analysis of your orders over the past year shows a steady growth, which means that within three months you will be needing 150,000 metres regularly. Deliveries are getting tighter and I don't want to let you down, so if you order now ...'

*　　*　　*

Both of these openings can lead to a quick close.

Question Opening:

'The trend seems to be to switch from transistors to minitors. How is that going to affect your production lines?'

'It could cause problems.'

'Well, here is a way we can help you.'

Question Opening:

'How are you being affected by the labour shortage in this area, Mr Jones?'

'It's getting worse every day.'

'Here is a way we can help you: Since I last called we have devised a pre-pack which will save you . . .'

*   *   *

Reference Opening:

'I called on your friend Brian Walker yesterday. He suggested that I should tell you about the results he is getting with Gripit. You haven't used it for some time now, Mr Brown, but I am sure you will want to consider it again.'

*   *   *

Sales Aid Opening:

'I have brought you our latest catalogue, Mr Lyons. It now gives a complete range of spare parts, which is in line with the suggestion you made a year ago. I'd like to show you . . .'

THE LINK OPENING

Have you see any TV thriller serials lately? If so, you will have noticed the regular use of the technique of showing a flashback from the final scene of the previous episode. It is this link with the past which immediately involves the viewer in the new episode.

The *Link Opening* in selling uses the same technique as the flashback on TV. A point discussed at one call becomes the link to hold the buyer's attention at the beginning of the next call.

Although the link technique can be used whatever the objective of the call back, it is most useful to those industrial salesmen whose products are repeatable and who, therefore, call on their buyers every four to six weeks, year in and year out.

'What can I say that is new,' they ask, 'when we have nothing exciting to offer for periods of six or nine months, or more?'

To these salesmen, the *link* helps maintain a continuing dialogue, the salesman probing, questioning, reminding, with the objective of selling strongly at every call, to get the maximum business *at every call*. Sometimes only a few words are needed—words most pleasing to a buyer—'You will remember what you said last time I called.' We are all anxious to hear our words of wisdom repeated.

If this *link* is not feasible the salesman can refer to a question left unanswered, a statement made by a third party, or a point made previously, in which the buyer has shown some interest.

For example:

'Mr Jones, you will remember that last month you said the problem of offcuts was becoming acute. I have been thinking very deeply about this point, and I want to suggest that . . .'

'Mr Smith, when I was here last week you told me of your plan to . . . This is how we can help your plan along . . .'

'Mr White, when I brought in your quotation last week I showed you the drawings, but I forgot to mention . . .'

There is one DON'T that every salesman should remember when working out a *Link Opening*. If, at a previous call, you have dealt with a complaint and settled that complaint, DON'T bring the matter up again by saying, 'Is the machine working all right now?' This will begin a trend of negative thoughts in the buyer's mind. If anything is wrong he will tell you, quickly enough.

Always recall *positive* points:

'Mr Johnson, last month you told me that it was essential for you to have the motors by 24th. Well they left for the site yesterday, 17th. As I promised, I was determined to give your order priority. But, Mr Johnson, deliveries will get progressively worse, and I feel sure now that you will want to . . .'

'I really appreciated the confidence you showed in me when I called last month and you told me of what was happening. *The Times* only published the news yesterday, but those three weeks have enabled us to draw up a new plan for you.'

'There was one point we touched on when I called last week, Mr Brown, and that was the noise factor. You said you were going to look into the question and, of course, with embossing machines the noise can sometimes be deafening. Now with our machines there is less noise than that of a typewriter.'

'Mr Bright, when I was here last week I promised to bring you a photograph of some of our non-ferrous castings, to give you some indication of how our experience can help you. I have had this photograph taken specially for you.'

GETTING ATTENTION

1. Never sell under adverse conditions.
2. Don't gabble; always speak slowly so that the buyer can hear every word.
3. Keep the *chat gap* as short as possible.
4. Make certain that you have worked out the best possible opening sentence, based on:
   (a) Factual Opening
   (b) Question Opening
   (c) Reference Opening
   (d) Sales Aid Opening
   (e) Demonstration Opening
5. When calling back, make sure that you get attention by using any of the standard openings, or a Link Opening.
6. Always remember, the objective of the opening is to obtain the undivided attention of the buyer.

12

Closing the Sale

Accuse any salesman of working for a competitor and he will have good grounds to sue you for slander, yet many a salesman does help his competitors to obtain orders. Although selling so well that a buyer becomes very interested in the total proposition, he doesn't attempt to close the sale. The buyer, in consequence, is able to consider alternatives, and one alternative could mean buying from a competitor.

At the end of a sales offer a buyer can say 'Yes', or 'No'. It is at this point that so often, he is allowed to get away with the delay excuse, 'I will certainly buy from you, but just leave it a few more days.'

Before the salesman calls back, a competitor—perhaps a very strong closer—may see that buyer with the advantage that the total proposition has already been sold for him. He need only concentrate on proving that his offer is tailored exactly to the buyer's needs to get the order.

There comes a time—perhaps on the first call, or even on the tenth call—when a buyer has complete understanding of the proposition—when he is obviously interested and able to buy. It is then that a salesman must determine to obtain a decision.

Many industrial salesmen, on losing an order, have said something like this:

> 'I'd have bet fifty to one I'd get that order. Everything was going fine—he even sent out for tea for us—then suddenly, at the very last minute, he changed his mind and told me he'd have to think it over, and I've learned what that means! In my line of country, if you don't get the order at the first real opportunity you've generally lost it. I don't know what the hell went wrong.'

Or, another bewildered salesman might say:

'I told everyone that that order for £50,000 was in the bag. I've called on Lawrence regularly over the two months since we first received the inquiry and, of course, I've known him for years. We carried out a survey and he congratulated me on the care taken. Also, I personally went to his factory to go through his equipment point by point with everyone concerned. After I'd posted the quotation I followed up with a telephone call and Lawrence told me that he'd never received a clearer quote or one better laid out. He promised to post us the order last Monday-week, and I got ready to celebrate on the Tuesday. It didn't arrive. I telephoned Wednesday and he said he was getting it off for sure on Thursday, but last Monday it still hadn't turned up and everyone at the office began ribbing me. I telephoned Lawrence again this morning and he told me the order had gone to Wetherby, our competitors. He explained that it wasn't his fault—that the order was all made out for us and then his managing director who, apparently, knows old man Wetherby very well, insisted that the business should be given to them. It's hardly credible, because they're five per cent more expensive than we are. It makes you want to weep for British Industry, doesn't it?'

Promises—Promises

Probably, because salesmen are usually optimists, they believe time after time in promises made by buyers or specifying authorities. It doesn't matter how often a salesman learns the bitter lesson—that buyers' promises can be broken—he will still say, 'This time I *know* we'll get the order.'

Too often, a salesman misinterprets a delay excuse for a promise. Buyers use such phrases as:

'I'm sure it will be all right.'

'Don't worry, you know I'll do my best.'

'Leave it to me.'

'If I have anything to do with it, you'll get the business.'

These are not promises, yet on such airy phrases a salesman

will telephone his sales manager excitedly to tell him that the order has been won.

All salesmen know that an order is not definite until it has been sanctioned, but they still delude themselves into believing that the latest negotiation is different—a 'certainty' for them.

Orders are not generally lost on the seventh, eighth, or ninth call, when a buyer gives some weak reason for not being able to place the order. The order is usually lost on the very first call— or on the first call back after a quotation has been submitted. At that first call, when the final decision is some way off there is no need for a buyer to be too difficult, he knows that he will be seeing other salesmen and studying their propositions. But, because at a first call a buyer is apparently receptive to a salesman's offer, the salesman sometimes forgets to sell, omitting to stress those extra benefits. Because that salesman believes the order is a mere formality, he doesn't resell when presenting the quotation, when there may still be doubts in the buyer's mind. Later, he wonders why he lost the order.

Sometimes quotations do not meet specifications. A supplying company may have a bad record for service, which weighs with a buyer; or they may employ a too keen credit controller, or may not keep to delivery dates; or the value offered is not as good as that offered by a competitor. There are many reasons why orders are lost, but so often, they are lost through bad salesmanship.

There is an old selling tag: *A good sale closes itself*. While this is not strictly true, it does apply quite often, always provided the salesman has not committed the selling sin of *stopping the buyer buying*.

There are four *stoppers* which cause salesmen to lose orders, not at the last moment, but early in the sale. Here they are:
1. talking on when the buyer is ready to buy
2. not listening
3. not giving proof
4. not getting agreement, step by step.

Talking on When the Buyer is Ready to Buy

When a salesman doesn't ask for a decision, but meanders on and on repeating himself over and over again, a buyer loses concentration. His mind wanders, and during its wandering it can light on the fact that a competitor might be able to make a better offer.

Not Listening

Will Rogers once said, *If you listen more you may learn something.* This really does apply to salesmen.

Sometimes a buyer raises a query or makes a comment which the salesman, being intent on selling, only half hears. But if a salesman doesn't give careful consideration to a buyer's viewpoint he may brush aside the one factor which could make or mar a sale. The buyer's mind then switches off and from then on he may nod his agreement, but he is thinking of other things. When the time comes to close the order this agreeable buyer says, 'I'll think it over.'

If a salesman is not certain whether he has heard a buyer's remark correctly he should ask him to repeat it.

'Would you just explain that point again, Mr Brown?'

Or, 'Have I got the point clear, Mr Smith, is it . . .?'

Are you a good listener? Do you listen with your eyes as well as with your ears? Do you watch a buyer's face to see if it is indicative of his feelings? Does it mirror the strength of the point he is making? Do you look directly at him, so that he knows you are paying attention to what he is saying?

The hallmark of the bad listener is that he shows his lack of interest by looking in every direction instead of at the buyer. Wandering eyes can mean nervousness, but more often than not this mannerism means lack of concentration. The non-listener not only misses vital points and brushes aside minor points, but he also annoys the buyer. Often a buyer has said (irrationally, of course), 'He couldn't have sold to me if he'd given me a thirty per cent discount—I didn't like his manner.'

In many instances the 'manner' referred to means that the salesman talked too much, and did not listen enough.

Try to think of someone you know who listens intently. Isn't he a likeable, popular person?

Now think of someone else who irritates and annoys you because he seems to want to monopolise the conversation. He's disliked, isn't he?

Not listening is a closing stopper because:

1. the salesman misses important points which indicate the buyer's real interest, or lack of it, in the sales offer;

2. the buyer, in his turn, becomes a non-listener, which the salesman believes indicates full acceptance of the offer. So when the buyer doesn't agree to purchase, the non-listener is baffled. He can't understand what went wrong at the last moment.

I hope he will now have that understanding.

Giving Proof

Buyers do not call industrial salesmen liars, but does that imply that the buyer believes every word he is told? Of course not! It only means that most buyers are courteous and see no sense in insulting a salesman. But all buyers do, on occasion, have reservations and doubts about claims made by salesmen—that is why they ask questions. (Objections will be covered in a later chapter.) These questions may arise from doubts. The salesman's answer can satisfy a buyer or leave him still dubious. Even when a buyer apparently agrees with the answer he is given, he can still have reservations—that is why every salesman should try to prove all major claims, and as many minor claims as possible.

A salesman might say, 'It's actually twenty per cent faster', or, 'Because of the linked switch it cannot cut out.' These are statements which a buyer may or may not believe. They should be proved by data explaining how the twenty per cent extra speed has been achieved and, perhaps, by a technical report from an independent authority to confirm that the linked switch does stop cut-outs.

Another point to remember is that although benefits are derived from facts which, in turn, are given YOU appeal, the

YOU appeal is not proof. For example, a salesman might say:

'The whole unit is made of butalin, which is lighter than aluminium and so the unit can be fixed on a wall. This means that it will only occupy half the space of your present machine and will need only one operator instead of two. This is a saving in time and money.'

Here we have a fact, plus two benefits. But what proof is there that butalin is lighter than aluminium? And if it is, how much lighter—5%—20%—50%? Also, the buyer will want to have proof that only one operator is needed instead of two. Without adequate proof he may not argue the point, but he will mentally discount the claim.

It is important to prove as many points as you can. Do not leave that data brochure in your case because you have used it so often that you now tend to neglect it. Pinpoint part of a report which proves a particular claim. Whatever your company has given you in the way of proof, whatever you have accumulated for yourself, should be used at every call. Never believe that a buyer will necessarily remember, six months later, the proof shown to him earlier.

When a sale is in the final stages and is then apparently lost, the real reason could be that proof was not given early, or not reiterated at a later call.

Not Getting Agreement Step by Step

For a salesman to be reasonably certain that only a gentle nudge will be needed to close the order, he must progress the sale from the opening to its conclusion. This, he achieves by constantly checking to make sure that the buyer understands, appreciates, and agrees with, every feature, every benefit, every claim made and is also satisfied with the proof given. This 'question' and 'agreement' technique is known as *getting responses*. Here are examples of the form the questions could take:

'Mr Johnson, you do agree, don't you, that the electronic shutter is right for your purpose?'

'It is essential for your requirements, isn't it, Mr Smith, that the area should be soundproof?'

'This advance in sophisticated micro-electronic techno-logy can save you endless problems—you agree, don't you, Mr Brown?'

'You'll admit, won't you, that the automatic switch will save you money?'

'You prefer the better quality paper then. . .?'

By getting a buyer's agreement all through the sale you are progressing towards an automatic close.

There should be no attempt to close an order early in the sales offer because a buyer looks interested—no professional buyer will order until he has heard a complete proposition. There are, of course, exceptions—for example, when a buyer needs and wants a product urgently, or when he has made up his mind to purchase in advance of the salesman's call. If a buyer knows that due to shortages he must stock up, or wants to buy because the prices are about to rise, he will show that he is in a buying mood. He is more friendly, will ask questions about deliveries, discounts for quantities, etc., may even take out an order book on the salesman's arrival. In this buying situation, a salesman should close as quickly as possible, to save his and the buyer's time.

With these exceptions, a sale should only be closed on the completion of the offer when the buyer, having heard all of the evidence, can make a decision. It is then that he will often signal his intention to order by asking pertinent questions.

These are the buying signals to look for at the end of the sales offer:

What he says:

'Let me check the size again.'

'I'm not sure about the finish—can you do it in . . .?'

'Will there always be spare parts available?'

'Are you sure that . . .?'

'Are you certain it won't . . .?'

What he does:

Studies the agreement and order form again.

Picks up the brochure/catalogue/report/data sheet and reads it very carefully.

Operates the demonstration model once more.

Picks up a sample and examines it closely.

Looks towards the place suggested for the installation of equipment.

Calls in a member of his staff and talks approvingly about your offer.

Ask

You have completed your sales offer and believe that you have interpreted a buying signal correctly. What can happen?

1. The buyer says, 'Right, I'll have it!' or words to that effect.
2. The buyer still hesitates, waiting for you to prompt him for a decision.

If you also hesitate he will regain his authority and say, 'Call again towards the end of next week. By then I shall have a chance to ... (speak to someone, see someone, think it over).'

3. You ask for the order.

The average salesman so rarely asks for a decision. This is due to timidity or fear. Being afraid of the reply 'No' he would rather create a prospect than risk losing the order. He is quite happy to be told to come back next week. He is content. There has been no victory, but neither has there been a defeat.

This fear of asking for the order must be overcome if a salesman is to succeed. Every buyer knows why salesmen are employed, and why they make calls: they want orders. Yet so many orders are lost because salesmen will not ask the direct question, 'May I have the order?'

It need not always be as direct as that, but even if it is, very few buyers will object.

The salesman may prefer to say:

> 'You can always telephone me regarding after sales service. Now let me note down the details.'

> 'I'll telephone the office straight away to have four units put aside for you.'

> 'I'm sure it will Mr Smith, so shall we get the details settled?'

'You will want it then, Mr Brown. If you'll give me an order number now I can start getting the order processed.'

If every salesman made up his mind to ask for the order at every opportunity (that is, of course, whenever a buyer is able to give the decision) he would break every target set by his sales manager.

CLOSING TECHNIQUES

There are many occasions when a hesitant buyer needs a 'nudge' before he will make up his mind, even after he has given buying signals. There are closing techniques which do enable a salesman to urge the buyer gently towards making his decision.

The Alternative Close

If a prospective buyer is hesitant and doesn't give a clear buying signal, there is a risk in asking directly for the order. He could reply 'Yes', but he could also say, 'No'. If the answer is 'No', the salesman is faced with the difficult task of persuading him to change his mind. By offering alternatives the salesman is not inviting a 'Yes' or 'No' he is only asking the buyer to tell him which of the alternatives he prefers. It is true he could answer, 'Neither!' But remember we are now dealing with the hesitant buyer, not with the one who has strong objections to buying. This buyer wants to buy but can't make up his mind, and only requires very gentle persuasion to help him arrive at a final decision.

Here are examples of *The Alternative Close*:

'The unit can be installed in that corner or close to the sorting machine—which do you prefer?'

'Would you prefer our cleaners to work early in the mornings, or after hours in the evenings?'

'Do you prefer the finish in grey or black?'

'Do you want us to hold pending instructions, or deliver to site?'

'Do you want us to deliver the truck, or would you rather collect it from our depot?'

'Do you want a solid fixing, or would you prefer the unit to be easily movable?'

'Do you require the extra long extension, or would our standard ten foot extension suit you better?'

When the buyer states his preference the salesman should accept his answer as denoting a willingness to buy, and should begin to note down details or ask for the order number.

The Summary Close

Have you a good memory? If so, you are very fortunate. Many people can't remember what *they* said two minutes ago, let alone what someone else told them. The majority would be hard put to remember everything they were told during a recent conversation. That is why defence and prosecuting counsels and the judge summarise for a jury, to remind them of all the facts of the case.

At the end of the sales offer the buyer may have forgotten a major benefit, so the salesman must remind him of all the major benefits that he has outlined during the sale.

For example:

'Mr Smith, our Chromart will give you so many benefits. First you will save your present dual costing system because it is a combined electronic calculator and typewriter. Second, invoices can be typed, additions made on the same machine, and discounts printed. Third, you will cut direct costs because when set at automatic you can produce statements from sets of invoices. And fourth, it will save you space, because it is smaller than a standard electric typewriter.'

'Mr Williams, I should like to sum up for you all the many advantages of Apex Automated Lathes:

One: the Apex will handle parallel and taper turning, drilling, and knurling.

Two: it will handle your continuous operations, including, of course, internal and external threading.

Three: a sophisticated programmer controls the hydraulically operated Apex.

Four: a programme allows for six cross slide and eight tail stock operations.

Five: your operator will be able to depend on a control panel which shows the cycle currently in operation.

'Mr Williams, I have stressed to you the benefits you will derive from each of these five features, but there is an additional one, which is that the Apex will cost you no more than any machine without these refinements. It only needs a power point, Mr Williams. Perhaps you would like to show me which one will be most convenient for you.'

The salesman would not list every benefit—that would be too time-consuming—but because he has previously stated the benefits he can, as in the example of the Apex Automated Lathe, restate only the main features and then turn them into a final benefit.

On completion, the salesman should always ask direct for the order, or offer alternatives.

Closing on a Minor Point

This is a form of trial close. The salesman has lost little if the minor point is not acceptable to the buyer. He can continue with his sales offer and try to close again later.

Here are examples of *closing on a minor point*:

'You do prefer the anti-corrosive finish, don't you, Mr Lock?'

'Would you like me to bring these drawings to you tomorrow morning?'

'Shall I arrange for an engineer to telephone you in the morning to talk about installation?'

'Don't you think it would be a change for the better, Mr Prior, if the print on the carton were changed from blue to red?'

'Do you like the idea of a pilot light being combined with a buzzer?'

When the buyer agrees on the minor point the salesman again accepts that the order is his, notes down details, or offers alternatives.

The Concession Close

There are occasions when a salesman is allowed to make a special concession to customers. For example, this could be when, normally, a standard quantity discount is allowed for orders of fifty units or more. As a special concession the salesman is permitted to offer this discount for only forty units. Or a guarantee could be extended from one year to two, as a boost for sales. Trading-in allowances might be increased; a survey for which a charge is usually made could be offered free; or there could be a special concession of a free supply of refills for machines. There could be a willingness to hold stocks to be drawn upon as required; or a guarantee to hold prices for six months; or free delivery to site. When a salesman is allowed to make such a special concession he usually uses it in his opening:

> 'Mr Jones, you will be pleased to hear that, for orders of
> three hundred units placed now, we will extend credit for
> six months without charging interest.'

Why should that please Mr Jones when, possibly, he doesn't know at that stage whether he will need to place so large an order, or if he can use up the supply within the six-month period? If he can buy at a similar price elsewhere and pay monthly for the goods he may still be better off than placing an order for three hundred.

Until a buyer is persuaded that all of the benefits offered, when added up, will make a purchase worth while for him, he may not be deeply interested in a special concession.

Even if a regular supplier offers a special concession, the buyer may try to get the concession without meeting the special demands of the supplier (taking immediate delivery; or a larger quantity; or stocking a new range of components).

It is so much wiser, therefore, to hold back the concession, and to use it to help close the order. Then, when the buyer is mentally weighing up the pros and cons of the offer—when, perhaps, benefits/costs stay equally poised—the salesman may tip the scales in his favour by saying,

'Mr Smith, I am sure that the range of adhesives will be of immense value to you, but as an extra incentive for you to buy now, I can give you . . .'

GET THE DECISION

You can use any combination of these closing techniques—you can summarise and then close on a minor point; you can offer a concession and then close on an alternative; but if you use these closing techniques in a positive manner, if you will always ask for the order, you will, undoubtedly, close more orders and get more decisions.

13

Overcoming Objections

Salesmen are sometimes given this advice:

> *Welcome objections, they prove that the buyer is interested and wants more information.*

Those who believe in welcoming objections obviously do not differentiate between *major* objections and *information-seeking* objections.

Consider these remarks by buyers:

1. 'In which way will your electronic unit cut down costs when, by using manual labour, we can have parts made inexpensively in areas where labour is readily available?'

2. 'You tell me how we can use your tubing, when it is two inches wider in diameter than we need.'

3. 'But what about the fire risks with Telopolin? I read in the paper . . .'

These are *information-seeking* objections and *are to be welcomed*, because they do show that the buyer is interested.

The first buyer wants to know how he can dispense with manual labour and use, profitably, electronically driven units.

The second buyer wants to be told how he can benefit by using the larger diameter tubing.

The third buyer wants to hear that the risks of Telopolin are minimal.

Yes, these buyers are definitely interested.

But no salesman should welcome *major* objections like:

> 'Now you listen to me—I'll say it again. It is cheaper for us to use the manual labour of small manufacturers. I'm not switching to electronics in any circumstances.'

> 'I have to work to specifications. Your inlet tube is two inches too large in diameter. Sorry, but it's no use to me.'

> 'Telopolin? Good God man, do you realise the fire risk if I were to use it in our factory? No thank you!'

Does any salesman really welcome this type of objection? But whether he welcomes it or not, a salesman has to close orders in spite of major objections or information-seeking objections; and here he faces a problem—how to avoid antagonising a buyer.

Imagine this scene:

> While making final plans before leaving for a holiday a husband says to his wife: 'We have to be at the airport an hour before take-off, so it's going to be a bit of a rush. We shall have to leave at nine o'clock.'
>
> 'No we needn't dear,' answers the wife, 'we can leave at half-past nine. We have to check in half an hour before take-off.'
>
> 'Look, I ought to know, I got the tickets, didn't I? The girl at Best's Travel told me—'
>
> 'Then she told you wrong, or you didn't hear what she said. I know it's half an hour because Gladys and her husband caught the same flight last week, and . . .'
>
> 'Oh for goodness sake, why do you always have to argue when I tell you I know? I was told . . .'
>
> 'You don't know, because you're making a mistake.'

The husband is about to lose his temper when suddenly it comes back into his mind that the girl at Best's Travel had said thirty minutes, and not sixty.

Now what does he do? Apologise immediately? Not likely! He either digs his heels in and insists that he's right, or walks out of the room murmuring, 'Women!' Then he has to work out ways of getting to the airport one hour before departure while ensuring that his wife doesn't make further inquiries and discover the truth.

None of us likes to be proved wrong, and this applies particularly to those with authority to buy. Yet if a buyer raises an objection, a salesman has to prove him wrong if there is to be any progress towards the close of the sale. And this must be achieved without an argument developing, without the buyer becoming annoyed, and without the salesman creating the impression that he is more knowledgeable than the buyer.

The best technique for overcoming this problem is not to let the objection arise.

Think again of the argument which developed between the man and his wife *after* he had told her that they had to be at the airport one hour before the flight.

If the wife had raised the issue herself and had been able to prove conclusively that the time lag was half an hour, she would have forestalled her husband's categorical statement. No argument would have developed, because the husband would not have *voiced* his belief, and it is what is *said* that matters—not what is *thought*.

Nobody minds switching thoughts—most of us do it all the time. As others talk, explain, lecture we often want to interrupt; but later when our doubts have been removed we are glad that we remained silent. Once we have spoken out we try to justify ourselves, right or wrong. When a buyer voices his objection it becomes doubly hard to persuade him to alter his mind, and he will sometimes use ridiculous arguments, rather than admit that he is wrong.

The objective of the salesman, when devising his sales offer, is to forestall major objections, so avoiding a subsequent clash of ideas with the buyer determined to prove his objection valid.

The first step in reaching this objective is to analyse objections; for only by a better understanding of the reasons for objections can a salesman forestall them.

ANALYSING OBJECTIONS

In the main, objections fall into two groups: *primary*, and *selective*. When a buyer cannot see a need for a product he raises a *primary* objection—he doesn't want to buy your product or service, or anyone else's.

For example, a managing director might decide that his company has no need for a computer. Time after time he will refuse appointments to computer salesmen, always using the *primary* objection, 'We have no need for a computer.'

When a buyer is in the market for a product and has only to

decide between competitive sales offers, he will raise with each competing salesmen *selective* objections.

Primary Objections

It is a complete waste of time to stress general benefits in the face of a *primary* objection. Nearly always when a *primary* objection is raised, there is an unrecognised need.

If a salesman knows that a need exists, he must plan to sell the need (not the product) in his opening sentence, and forestall the *primary* objection.

Let us consider again the example of the managing director who believes his company has no need of a computer. The salesman who plans carefully uses these opening words:

'Mr Johnson, many of my clients would not have given a moment's consideration to purchasing a computer even a year ago, but companies like AYZ changed their views when they heard that a daily stock figure could be produced within an hour by using our inexpensive midget computer. And with money so dear . . .'

Because that managing director suddenly realises the saving to him by having a quick daily stock check, and because he wants to know why the AYZ board changed its views when they heard of the new midget computer, he allows the salesman to continue with the sales offer.

The success of this technique for dealing with a *primary* objection depends on the ability of the salesman to work out an appropriate opening.

The Selective Objection

Objection analysis is necessary if a salesman is to forestall major objections. The first step in this exercise is to consider objections raised by buyers, but because all buyers do not raise the same one, a complete list of all *selective* objections, major and minor, should be prepared. These will cover a wide field: price—design—size—weight—noise—durability—running costs—not up to standard specification—not passed by an authority (fire department, insurance, etc.)—difficulty in fixing—supplier not carrying out installation—satisfied with present supplier—storage problems—handling problems—workers against its use—past problems (customers let down over service, delivery, etc.).

The next step is to decide on the best answers to each objection listed.

Forestalling the Objection

The completed list of objections and answers should now be studied in conjunction with the sales offer analysis forms. Consider each feature/benefit to determine whether or not the YOU appeal sentence should be altered to counter a possible objection.

For example, you are selling a piece of equipment which is noisy and an objection to the noise is raised at nearly every call. There is, however, a good reason for the noise. To quieten the unit would entail extra costs and in the opinion of the marketing director, the benefits you can offer far outweigh the noise factor. The noise is due to a mechanism which helps considerably to reduce the consumption of oil, while at the same time working at a faster rate, and improving production. The design team felt there was no point in losing these advantages for the sake of quietness but the objection arises time and time again, and is difficult to overcome in spite of the extra benefits offered.

In your sales offer you have already stressed the benefits of reduced oil consumption, etc., but the buyer having, perhaps, been primed by a competitor might say,

'That's all very well, but what about our operators who will have to stand by the machine all day? The noise will drive them up the wall.'

What you have to do is slightly to change the YOU appeal benefit sentence, before the objection arises.

You might say something like this:

'Mr Jones, the Star equipment, as you probably know, has been specially designed to give you reduced consumpion of oil while at the same time, stepping up production—and this is achieved without excessive noise. We haven't silenced the unit at your expense as we could so easily have done. This would only have added to the cost for no real purpose.'

You will not, then, pause for comment by the buyer, but continue to prove the savings, and later, seek a 'Yes' response. Having put the issue in its true perspective, the molehill of noise has not become a mountain—a crescendo of sound—in the buyer's mind. When you re-emphasise the saving in cost due to the rational thinking of your design, or R & D department, you take the sting out of a competitor's claim while discounting the noise factor. If it were not for the competitor's claims the buyer would, perhaps, not have raised the objection at all.

Although the buyer may have the noise factor in mind when the salesman begins his sales offer, he can change his mind while the salesman is stressing the advantages of the unit. If the objection has been successfully forestalled, the buyer may think along these lines:

'We're always getting complaints about noise and draughts—or it's too hot, or too cold. It's probably no noisier than the hydraulics in B shop.'

It is worth remembering that nearly everyone exaggerates when attempting to prove a point, and buyers, especially, are prone to exaggerate. When a buyer tells you that the price is 20% too high, he usually means about 5%. When he tells you that he can get delivery from X by return, he probably means in two weeks but he will buy from you if you can do better.

To get a realistic figure you should always, mentally, tone down a buyer's claim.

Imagine, now, that you are selling vending machines to be installed on the factory floor, available for use at any time of the day. You will often meet the standard objection:

'That's not for us! Why, they'd be crowding round the machine all day—the loss of time would be much too high.'

You can forestall this objection by saying:

'Mr Williams, the great advantage of installing these machines on the factory floor is that you will maintain production. As you know, Mr Williams, during the day there are always fatigue times when, however conscientious men may be, they begin to feel weary and ease off. When they are allowed to have a quick cup of tea or coffee you will find the fatigue time will be eliminated. But I know exactly how you feel, Mr Williams, you can imagine a day-long queue by the machine—and this will happen to a small extent, for the first day or so. After that, experience proves that no more time is taken up when the machines are in use than by normal break periods. That is why they have been installed by X, by Y, and by Z. Think of the benefit to you of having these machines on the shop floor— better industrial relations and no falling off of output during peak fatigue hours.'

If you are selling tubing, you might be met regularly with the objection:

'*I can get exactly the same from X, there is no need for me to open a new account.*'

Once more, you may want to forestall the objection. You could say:

'Mr King, I am not claiming that our tubing is less expensive or more expensive than any other—but I can claim that with us you are assured of outstanding service, which has to be experienced to be appreciated.'

By emphasising early in the sales offer the outstanding service your company gives, you may remind a buyer that the standards of his present suppliers are not as good as they may have been in the past.

Many salesmen regularly meet the objection:

'*I want immediate delivery—I can get them quicker elsewhere.*'

If you know that you cannot deliver your products quickly, it would be wrong to make rash promises. You can forestall the objection in this way:

'I know, Mr Thomas, that you want deliveries as quickly as possible—but I also know that nothing would get past you if it were not manufactured to the highest standards. Our quality product has to pass through six separate tests. When we deliver in nine weeks' time you will not need to put them through any tests yourself they are guaranteed by us. . . .'

You will never attempt to forestall every objection; you should try to forestall only those objections which either you meet time and time again, or which you know will be raised by the buyer you are calling upon.

Your object is *not* to put controversial issues in the buyer's mind, but to forestall major objections.

The Brush-Off Objection

Here are examples:

'I'm seeing no more salesmen today.'

'I'm not interested, thank you.'

'I'm far too busy to discuss this matter now.'

This form of objection may be met even when the interview is by appointment.

Here are the standard answers:

'I'm so sorry I caught you at the wrong moment but . . .'

'It is because you are so busy that you will be interested in . . .'

'It's my fault, Mr Smith. Obviously, I haven't made it clear . . .'

Unfortunately, these answers rarely work—although they should be tried. When a salesman meets a quick brush-off it is sometimes better for him to leave, research to discover what the buyer really needs, and return with an opening more suitable to those needs. On a subsequent visit he may find the buyer in an entirely different mood.

There is often a reason for the quick brush-off, especially if an appointment has been made. Assuming that the salesman has not annoyed the buyer in any way by his manner, bearing, the words he uses or the clothes he wears, it may be that the buyer has just had 'one of those days'—problems with the staff, problems with the managing director, or he might have been reprimanded, his budget may have been cut, perhaps he has had a quarrel with his wife before leaving for the office.

It is almost an adverse selling situation, but not quite. If the salesman is always aware that a brush-off is possible he can plan to meet it by having ready in his mind a special benefit to suit that particular buyer.

He can say,

> 'Of course, I won't worry you this morning. But may I leave you with one thought: Our Nufix will take away *all* risk of an electrical breakdown.'

One key sentence such as this can change a brush-off into an invitation to stay. Although the buyer may be in a black mood or his mind may be occupied with other matters, he *is* a buyer, and if he has experienced problems which the salesman suggests can be overcome, he may quickly change his mind and want to hear more.

The Delay Objection

The delay objection is not, on the face of it, an objection to buying, but to arriving at an immediate decision.

Here are examples:

> 'I want to think again about the fixing problem. Come and see me next week.'

> 'I'll have to see my partner, as he is involved in the design of this job.'

> 'It's a bit over the price limit so I'll have to put it before the Board.'

> 'Although your offer seems right there are other factors that I have to consider. One of them is that I must have other quotations.'

> 'As it might mean a change in our production line I shall have to speak to R & D first.'

> 'As it is partly to do with transport I shall have to discuss it with Mr Neville.'

When, just before the moment of decision, a buyer says, 'I must see Mr Neville about this', it is nearly always an excuse to delay the decision. Otherwise, very early in the sale (and this applies especially if the negotiations have taken place over a long period) he would have told the salesman that Mr Neville would have to be involved. In fact, a buyer, if interested in a proposition, will gladly arrange a meeting between the salesman and anyone else who may be involved in the buying decision.

For all that, a salesman cannot accept a delay excuse and walk out. He must try for the full support of the buyer if Mr Neville is to be convinced. He should say something like this:

> 'I appreciate that Mr Neville must be consulted, but if, at this moment, the decision were solely yours, would you place the order?'

If the buyer is hesitant or gives a negative reply, the salesman will know that he has not proved his case. He will then have to discover the real reason why the buyer will not arrive at an immediate decision. Generally, however, the buyer using a delay objection is using the excuse to avoid making a decision. He is not sure – he wants to think it over. But what is there for him to think over if he has been given a complete sales offer in an hour, a day, a week, or over a period of weeks or months? The thinking time is when he is with the salesman. That is when he can ask questions, and clear his mind of doubts. We know, therefore, that most delay objections are not valid. The problem facing the salesman is to discover a buyer's real reason for delaying his decision.

All delay objections, if genuine, are raised early in the sale. When discussing design a buyer will tell the salesman that this is a subject that he will have to discuss with the R & D department, or with a project engineer. A change in the production line will obviously involve others—possibly trade union officials. But if these delay reasons (not objections) are *not* made clear early in the sale, the buyer usually doesn't have to delay buying. If he is apparently satisfied on all points of the sales offer but still says, 'Leave me a leaflet (catalogue, drawing, etc.)', then he is, most certainly, not satisfied with one or more of the features of the product or service.

There is, then, always a reason for the delay excuse, and the reason is usually one that the buyer doesn't want to disclose to the salesman.

It is a *hidden objective*.

The Hidden Objection.

Yes, buyers do hide their true objections from salesmen, time and time again. That is why they occasionally seem to act irrationally.

What perturbs a salesman is that in spite of a good presentation which gets 'Yes' responses, a buyer will say, 'No, leave it for a week or so.' At such a moment many salesmen do not know what action to take. They have answered every objection that the buyer has raised except one—the one the buyer is hiding from them.

It is said of Talleyrand the French diplomat, well versed in the double talk of politicians, that when he was told that a foreign envoy would not be arriving at a conference for the very good reason that he had died on the way there, Talleyrand answered, 'Yes, but I wonder what was the real reason for his not coming.'

Let us first consider what a salesman can do to find the real reason for the delay objection.

He can say,

> 'I appreciate, Mr Johnson, that you would like to leave the matter over for two or three weeks, but what is there to think over? Perhaps I haven't explained everything clearly.'

To which he will nearly always receive the reply, 'No, you have done very well, everything is very clear—just leave it for now.'

When a salesman knows early in the sales offer that someone else is involved in the buying decision he will, of course, ask to be allowed to see that person (committee, board). But when he is not sure of the validity of the objection he might say:

> 'Mr Jackson, forgive me if I take up another ten seconds of your time blowing my own trumpet. I have been with my company some time, as you know, and I not only had six months of intensive training, but have attended refresher courses every year. This enables me to give a better service to our customers, and also to explain fully every facet of our product. Do you think it fair, Mr

Jackson, for a board (committee, associate) to have to arrive at the correct decision without having these facts? I know you will do everything you possibly can for me, but I am a specialist in this particular field.'

The answer will, invariably, be, 'You can leave it to me. I have all the facts at my finger tips, and I promise I'll do the best I can for you.'

He won't, because he is not sure himself whether or not he should buy. He has an objection unanswered, because he has hidden it from the salesman.

The effective technique you can use to find the hidden objection is to invite the buyer to finish a sentence—a sentence which, instinctively, he will assume is based on knowledge.

When a buyer is unexpectedly asked to voice a thought in this way you will hear the truth, more often than not.

Your technique is also based on a key phrase:

'And your *other* reason for not deciding now is. . .?'

Look straight at the buyer while you are speaking, and begin the sentence on a low note, finishing with a slightly higher inflection.

This technique must not be used at any time other than at the close. It would be quite wrong to seek the hidden objection earlier in the sale, when the buyer has not heard the complete sales offer. Also, the exact words must be used. To change them to, 'Is there any other reason for your delaying buying?' would inevitably, bring a negative reply. The direct question which invites a 'Yes' or a 'No' will usually get a 'No.'

If a salesman is continually meeting a delay objection it is because:

1. The sales offer is incomplete.

2. The salesman does not ask for the order. When the time arrives he is too timid to request a decision, leaving it to the buyer to say something—and the buyer usually raises a delay objection.

3. The salesman has not built confidence. Then the buyer, in his turn, becomes timid and fearful of making a mistake, and so delays matters.

4. There is a hidden objection which he has not been able to answer.

The Price Objection

There is no magic answer to the buyer who says, 'You are too expensive, I can buy cheaper.'

There are, of course, selling platitudes which are used regularly by salesmen, but which rarely work. For example:

> 'Do you always buy the cheapest, Mr Jones—the cheapest suit, the cheapest car. . .?'
>
> 'Nothing is so expensive as something that is cheap.'
>
> 'There is nothing manufactured that someone else cannot produce cheaper.'

Although these often repeated sentences rarely help, well thought out answers are essential in helping to overcome a price objection. But first a salesman should study the reasons why buyers react unfavourably to price and, equally important, he must analyse his own thinking on the whole subject.

The Salesman and the Price Objection

Under normal trading conditions most salesmen face price objections continually, not necessarily because a buyer believes he can buy cheaper, but because he wants to obtain a discount if possible. Unfortunately, however, too many salesmen believe that they have been singled out and their products condemned because of the pricing policies of their companies.

Is there a sales manager anywhere in the world who has not been told by a salesman that the company's product is being priced out of the market? (Our training organisation has associate companies in forty countries, and the same price objection is always of the most concern to salesmen.) Sometimes a salesman's fear of price is quite irrational, but while positive thinking won't help him much, 'my price is *not* too high, my price is *not* too high, my price is *not* too high'—negative thinking, 'my price is too high, everyone knows my price is too high' is disastrous.

Firstly, then, every salesman should decide how to defeat his own fear of the price objection. He should begin by asking himself two questions:

> 'Would my company still be in existence if our products were so over-priced?'

> 'As I have been taking orders at our standard prices, why should these buyers be so incompetent as to buy from me if they could buy better elsewhere?'

The next step in defeating the price bogey is for a salesman to meet a salesman employed by one of his competitors. This is not difficult, because salesmen meet each other all the time, on trains, in waiting rooms, in car parks and so on.

He should ask the other salesman this question:

> 'Why do you always undercut your prices?'

Back will come the reply, instantly:

> 'Well, I like that! My company undercut prices? That really is the pot calling the kettle black. It's your people who keep reducing the prices.'

If only salesmen could attend sales conferences of other companies in any field of activity they would find that at question time someone always raises and condemns the pricing policy. A salesman is rarely singled out for a price objection. It happens to everyone, but while some salesmen wait, almost expectantly, for the *blow* of a price objection, the successful salesman is quite proud that he does not compete on price, but competes very strongly on value.

He will say to a buyer, 'Not only does the Comet give you all these benefits, but in addition we guarantee a twenty-four-hour service. And the price is *only* . . .' because he believes that the price is relatively low compared with the value he is offering.

Remember, it is always value which determines the price the buyer will pay.

The Buyer and the Price Objection

It is a buyer's function to spend his company's money to the best advantage. His first consideration is to fill the exact need at the lowest possible price.

To achieve his aim his thoughts may conflict with the objections he voices. For example,

A buyer says: 'You are twenty per cent too dear.'

He thinks: *'It's about five per cent more than Brown's offer, but it will have a longer life, and that saves constant changes. I'll try to get him down in price. If not, I'll buy anyway.'*

A buyer says: 'You are much too expensive for our needs.'

He thinks: *'I have had so much trouble with Smith's, perhaps I should change over—pay a little more and get something more reliable, and save myself some headaches as well.'*

A buyer says: 'I can show you competitive quotes and you'll see that you are way out.'

He thinks: *'Those people do give world-wide service, and that's what our export people have been asking for, for a long time.'*

If the minds of these buyers could be read, the salesmen could so easily close the sales by

1. re-stressing the value of the long life of the product;
2. stressing the quality of the product;
3. stressing the value of world-wide service.

It is said that a dog can tell instinctively if a human being is afraid. Buyers certainly have a sense which tells them whether or not they can take advantage of a salesman's fear of price.

Buyers have told us over and over again that although they always feel it is part of their job to raise the price objection, they are also sending out a challenge: *'Convince me that it is in my interests to pay your price.'*

When to Introduce the Price

It is possible on many occasions to forestall a price objection if a salesman is able to heap benefit on benefit before he gives the price. Although that should be his aim, whenever he is asked the price by the buyer, he must not stall. Hesitation could be taken as a reluctance to give the price because it is too high.

The only exception to this rule is if the price cannot be given until a survey has been made and additional information obtained, or if it is necessary to have a better understanding of a buyer's exact needs. Only then may the salesman answer: 'I can't tell you exactly now, because ...' or, 'The price will depend on ...'

His objective, however, must be to give as many benefits as possible *before* introducing, or being asked the price.

Answering the Price Objection

Whether the price objection is used by a buyer to attempt to obtain an extra concession, or in the genuine belief that he could buy better, handling the objection is the same. The salesman must concentrate the mind of the buyer on price difference.

For example, a salesman quoting ten units at a total price of £1,200 may be told by the buyer that he could purchase similar units for £1,100.

The salesman says:

> 'Mr Jones, it is true our price is £120 a unit, and the price you want to pay is £110 a unit but, Mr Jones, think what you will get for that extra £10—and *it is only* £10 a unit. First, we guarantee ...'

The salesman would then stress the advantage of his product over any similar product the buyer could purchase.

Always pinpoint the *difference* in price—is it 5%, or 10%? Is it £10 or £20, £200 or £20,000? Nearly every buyer will give some indication of the price he will pay unless, of course, he is considering tenders. Assuming that the difference arrived at is £500 of the total quotation, the salesman must set out to prove the extra value the buyer would receive for *only* £500.

THE LOYALTY OBJECTION

This objection will be met by nearly all salesmen selling repeatable products (component parts, chemicals, oils, packaging materials, accessories, etc.). It is usually only encountered at a first call and is possibly the most difficult of all objections to overcome.

Here are buyers' reasons for their reluctance to change suppliers:

1. 'We have been with Smith & Co., for thirty years. I've been dealing with them myself for fifteen years, and before that our managing director who, in those days did his own buying, formed a friendly relationship with Tom Smith. They have always given us good service, so there is no point in my changing suppliers at the moment. Of course, if ever things altered . . .'

2. 'We are one of Brown & Co.'s largest customers, and no doubt because of that they look after us very well. We have only to telephone and they do everything to give us express delivery, submit samples, or accept the return of unsuitable goods. If ever they should let me down I shall be prepared to consider . . .'

3. 'It's a case of we buy from them—they buy from us. That's fair enough, isn't it? I can see no point in changing.'

These objections stem not so much from loyalty, although this does play a part, as from confidence in a supplier who has given good service over a number of years. Why should a buyer change when, over a period of time, he has had no real cause for complaint? He will only make an immediate change if another supplier can offer equal value plus extra benefits—better price, better delivery, better design, something new. With repeatable products a sudden great advantage of one supplier over another is rare, but no salesman can admit defeat when meeting this very difficult objection, and there are practical actions that he can take.

Firstly, he must remember the selling axiom:

When all things are equal the buyer buys from the salesman he likes the best.

This axiom should remind him to check on himself, not because his aim is to ingratiate himself with a buyer, but to make sure that he does not annoy the buyer in any way. That could be a mistake made by the opposition, especially if they change their salesman on the territory.

In any event, over a number of years, regular suppliers are apt to take a buyer for granted, while if they employ a new-comer to the territory he may not know—or may forget—that his objective at each call is to sell. He may become lackadaisical or off-hand, and antagonise not only the buyer, but also other members of the staff.

A salesman's efforts to please a buyer may not result in an order on the first call, third, fifth or sixth call, but eventually, the buyer's mind can be influenced by the salesman's friendly personality and by his enthusiasm—and because of his obvious keenness to obtain the business.

If salesmen could hear buyers talking to their staff they might well hear something like this:

> 'I rather like that fellow—he's keen, persevering, and always tries to be helpful. We'll give him a break one day.'

Here are some other positive steps the salesman can take:

1. He must have an objective at each visit, and never make the call hoping that something will turn up—the *'anything for me today?'* type of approach.

2. Even at the risk of being boring, at each call he should say to the buyer something like this:

> 'I really do appreciate the reason for your loyalty to Smith & Co., but as I have told you before, Mr Jones, it is my ambition for us to have the opportunity as Smith's had so many years ago—the opportunity to prove to you that we can offer a similar and, I feel sure, a better service.'

Or,

> 'Mr Harvey, it is impossible to read the future, but imagine a tragedy happening—perhaps a part of Smith's factory being burned down. Fires happen all the time—or there could be a strike. Wouldn't you like to know that in such an event you had another trusted supplier to help you over a difficult period? Naturally, when things were right again you would want to return to Smith's and that, of course, is fair. We are only aiming for a part of your business. If you will just test us now under normal conditions you will prove for yourself that . . .'

To obtain a share of worthwhile business from a buyer who refuses to open a new account, a salesman needs patience and perseverance. He must sell on each call, and sooner or later he will get that business.

Why?

Because the majority of salesmen calling on that buyer give up too readily, or make a series of 'anything for me today?' calls.

TECHNIQUES FOR HANDLING OBJECTIONS

1. *Don't interrupt.* All too often salesmen do not allow buyers to complete their objections. Because a salesman is so sure that he knows what the buyer is thinking, and believes that he has the answer, he interrupts, and by doing so, never hears the objection in detail.

For example, the buyer might say, 'Yes, that's all very well, but the lining . . .'

The salesman, feeling sure that the buyer is concerned about the strength of the man-made fibres used in the lining, interrupts with,

> 'Please don't worry about the lining, Mr Green. We can strengthen it by using an interlining as well.'

By saying this, the salesman may have put into the buyer's mind a query about the quality of the lining when, perhaps, he had only wanted to criticise its texture, colour or finish.

The buyer should always be allowed to state his objection in full. He must not be interrupted, and equally important, the salesman must look as though he is interested. His demeanour must not suggest that he has heard it all before, and is eager to give the answer.

No one likes a *too clever* person, and when salesmen interrupt with pat answers, they may appear to be too clever and may, in consequence, lose their buyer's confidence.

Always listen carefully to the buyer's complete objection, and then he will listen to your answer.

When an objection has been dealt with, do not return to it later in the sales offer.

For a salesman to be certain that he fully understands an objection it is sometimes wise to repeat it.

2. *The Apparent-Agreement Technique.* We know that a relaxed buyer decides more readily. We know that tensions build up in a buyer just before he comes to a decision, and often prior to his raising an objection.

He makes his point and waits for the skirmish to begin. But no salesman wants a battle, and if he is unable to forestall the objection he must try to remove the tension from the buyer. By using the *apparent-agreement* technique he indicates that he is inclined to agree with the objection, and the buyer thinks that he has won his point and relaxes.

Remember that the salesman only *apparently* agrees. If an objection is raised that the price is too high and the salesman answers, 'Yes, it is high but . . .' the buyer may relax, but the salesman will find it very hard to convince that buyer that the price is right, having once agreed with him. The emphasis is on *apparently* agreeing.

For example,

'I can understand, Mr Jones, your thinking at this stage that the extra investment may not be worthwhile, but . . .'

The salesman is only showing the buyer that he understands his way of thinking, but he is not agreeing with him.

'On the face of it, Mr Smith, it does seem right that extra labour might be needed, but . . .'

'Your concern about the viscosity of the oil, Mr Johnson, is understandable, but . . .'

'I quite see your point of view, Mr Green, I'm glad you raised it, but . . .'

Remember, the *apparent agreement* technique relaxes the buyer; slows down the pace of the sale; does not make the salesman appear to be too clever; and shows courtesy, because the salesman appreciates the buyer's point of view.

14

Selling through Specifying Authorities

Sometimes salesmen cannot obtain orders by directly influencing the buyer, but have to work through an independent intermediary who must be persuaded to instruct the buyer to purchase their product. Such an intermediary is a *specifying authority*.

Brian Moss, managing director of Nu-aire (Contracts) Ltd, has a long experience of selling through specifying authorities, and his sales team are outstandingly successful in this area of marketing.

He writes:

> The eventual user of the product may or may not be either the specifying authority or a buyer.
>
> When a local authority engineer specifies a product for use by that authority, the specifier and the user are one and the same; the purchase being made directly by the authority or by an independent firm working on its behalf. But when an architect instructs a builder to use a certain product for the eventual benefit of a tenant, the specifier, the buyer, and the user, are totally separate agencies. It is only the buyer and the specifier who are always independent of each other.

In both of these examples the specifying authority and the user are separated only by the buyer. In practice, the situation can be more complex, and the chain connecting the specifier to the user can be very much longer. For instance, the salesman selling air-conditioning equipment for use in a new hotel can find that the specifying authority—the *mechanical services consulting engineer*—is separated from the person who benefits from the equipment—the *hotel guest*—by the following agencies:

1. architect
2. mechanical services sub-contractor

3. main contractor
4. developer
5. hotelier

This specifying chain does not affect basic selling principles, but it does require the salesman to determine who makes and who influences decisions, and what will motivate those persons to use his equipment. In many cases, several people may be in a position to influence the specifying authority, and concentrating attention on the specifier only is, therefore, wrong. But as each of those interested in the product may have different, sometimes conflicting interests, their needs and motivating forces must be identified.

The salesman faced with a long or complex specifying chain must understand that different people buy or specify the same product from the same supplier for different reasons (see Chapter 6, page 57). What is of great appeal to one decision maker or influencer may be of little interest to another.

For example, the salesman selling air conditioning for a new hotel may have to analyse the features and benefits of an air diffuser (a grille through which air passes into an area).

Hotel guests will be the most impressed with the ingenious design, which prevents draughts causing them discomfort.

Motivating benefit—*health*.

Hotel management may be swayed by the easily removable core, allowing the normal maintenance staff to service and clean the diffuser.

Motivating benefit—*utility*.

Developers who are concerned with producing buildings of good value for their clients are more likely to be motivated by the inexpensive price of this diffuser.

Motivating benefit—*saving of money*.

Main contractors are not affected by the price of diffusers, nor are they particularly concerned about cleaning problems, but they are responsible for providing the builders' work fixings for the diffuser, and therefore, are favourably impressed because the diffuser requires very simple builders' work.

Motivating benefit—*saving of money*.

Services contractors often spend lengthy periods on site adjusting grilles and diffusers, and are responsible for correctly balancing the air distribution system. The factory-adjusted diffuser transfers this balancing responsibility to the manufacturers.

Motivating benefit—*protection and security*
Architects strive to produce attractive buildings, and a good looking diffuser.

Motivating benefit—*satisfaction of pride*.
Consulting engineers have to design systems which produce the required air conditions within certain cost and space limitations. A low resistance diffuser requires smaller, less expensive plant.

Motivating benefit—*efficiency*.

No salesman would, or could, contact each and every one of the links given in the example, but he certainly should interview as many as possible. Obviously, the salesman would not limit himself to the prime benefits, but would include subsidiary appeals in each case.

Often it is not a product, but a company feature, which should be emphasised. For instance a *design service* saving the architect or engineer time and money reduces his responsibility. Or a team of *service engineers* able to guarantee twenty-four-hour service may be a strong motivating factor.

What Specifying Authorities Have in Common

In the main, specifiers name products on which they know they can depend. Their aim is a design which works reliably at a reasonable price. They tend also to name firms of repute and to be guided by salesmen in whom they have confidence.

As technology advances and becomes more complex it is difficult, if not impossible, for even the most competent specifiers to keep abreast of all the latest developments. They therefore tend to rely—perhaps unwittingly—on salesmen to keep them up to date and to enable them to select and specify the most appropriate equipment. The salesman whose advice is sought has succeeded in *gaining the specifier's confidence*—the first step towards being specified, and eventually getting the order.

How to Sell to Specifiers

The only way the salesman can ensure that he presents his product in an appealing manner to each of the links in the specifying chain is to prepare well constructed presentations, enumerating the prime and subsidiary benefits of the product in such a way that they influence the listener.

This appears to be no different from the task facing any salesman, but there is one important factor which does make the task of the salesman calling on specifiers different from others. In this type of selling the salesman is calling on the same people week after week, month after month, and in many cases, year after year. The result is that too often, salesmen drift into unstructured conversations. This is one of the reasons for a notice outside offices reading:

REPRESENTATIVES WILL NOT BE SEEN WITHOUT AN APPOINTMENT.

Architects and engineers are forced to adopt this measure because too much of their time has been wasted by pointless, unplanned, meetings. They will often, however, see a salesman who they know, from previous calls, talks concisely and objectively about his product, who helps them with their problems, and who does not waste their time.

There is only one effective way to construct an interview. The salesman must *set his objectives* clearly for each call he makes—to meet someone who is not already known—to clear a problem—to deliver drawings or quotations—to obtain an inquiry—to discuss new products or to bring literature up to date.

Until the salesman sets his objective he cannot construct his presentation, and if he does not use such a presentation to structure the interview, the meeting will inevitably lapse into a time-wasting exercise.

Because the salesman is selling technical products, he must obviously be technically able. He must know his product—when it can be used, how it can be used, and also when it cannot be used. He must be able to discuss the product in the specifier's own terms, and must appreciate its ramifications and, if applicable, the effects on systems incorporating the product.

The salesman must be careful to ensure that this product is used correctly by the specifier, otherwise not only will the product and the manufacturer become discredited but the failure will tarnish the reputation of the specifier.

Sometimes the salesman is able to call on his own company's design and drawing office staff, but if these services are not available he should not reject simple felt-pen sketches, which are so effective when selling to the visually orientated personnel who make up the technical specifier's office.

The salesman must ensure that his company's catalogues are kept up to date, and that specifiers are aware of product changes. This responsibility often provides a splendid opportunity to the salesman to remind the specifier of his range of products.

Official Approval

Technical designers prefer to use products that have been approved by authorities. In the building trade these could be building inspectors, public health inspectors, or perhaps the local authorities themselves. The salesman who volunteers to visit these agents on behalf of the specifier in order to gain clearance for a new product, either for general use or for a particular contract, saves the specifier time and avoids his being embarrassed by not knowing the answers to questions the authorities may raise. Also, the specifier is more likely to try the product after the salesman has gained its approval and has shown that he is willing to help in such a practical way. The effort can, in any case, be valuable because it brings the salesman into contact with people who can be very helpful to him with other work. Business can result from the recommendations of inspectors to firms who inquire about the salesman's (and similar) products.

The Specification

The goal of the salesman selling to specifying authorities is to have his company's product uniquely written into the specification. Being uniquely specified in this way guarantees that his product will be used. However, many specifying authorities are not allowed to specify one company's products or as a matter of policy do not do so. They will name either a number of acceptable companies, or one company followed by the words *or equal and approved*.

In these instances the power is transferred from the specifying authority to the buyer who eventually places the order, and this more often than not results in a battle between those companies who are approved.

The salesman operating under these conditions can still put his company in a strong position when dealing with the eventual buyer. He can do this by having his company's product shown on the drawings, or described in such detail in the specification, that it would cost the buyer too much effort and money to go elsewhere.

As more and more specifications carry alternative names, so it becomes more and more important for the salesman to ensure that his product is the one which forms the basis for the specification and drawings.

The drawings and specifications produced by one specifying authority can also be important to another specifying authority, and it could well be that it is this latter specifier who, in the end, calls the tune. For instance, a drawing produced by a structural engineer is often the one which will finally determine what mechanical engineering product will be used by the mechanical engineering sub-contractor.

Here is an example which illustrates this most important point:

Roof fans sit on an upstand constructed on the roof by the main contractor. As there is a wide variety of upstand shapes and sizes, there is often confusion on site because the wrong type of stand is built. The roof fan salesman can bring out this point when speaking to the mechanical services specifier and can offer to visit the structural engineer and help him detail these upstands, so avoiding trouble for all. Obviously, both specifiers are quite happy about this situation because it is a guarantee that this particular detail will not give them problems later on.

In due course the sub-contractor will ask for tenders and will, in most cases, attempt to use the company which puts forward the lowest total price. However, if he attempts to use a roof fan which requires a different upstand size he will have to ask the main contractor to alter his drawings and construction details. The main contractor's attitude will be quite simple. Unless there is profit for him he will not spend time and money in changing drawings and, therefore, the sub-contractor will be forced to use the roof fan whose upstand was originally detailed.

A similar situation arises when an electrical engineer produces wiring diagrams which suit only one manufacturer's products, or if hydraulic or pneumatic connections and circuits are unique. In each case, these specifying authorities are unlikely to change their drawings because another trade concerned in the contract wishes to change the choice of product.

This means that the salesman who wants his product to be the basis of the specification must call on the specifier *when he is about to prepare the drawings and specification*. Only in this way can he ensure that another company's product is not substituted for his own.

The salesman should, therefore, have a system of records and information directing him to call at certain times to discuss certain jobs with certain people. He must call at the correct time, because if he is too early or too late it is quite possible that the specifying authority will draw in a competitive product.

The competent salesman will constantly progress jobs to show that he has the specifier's interests at heart and wants to make sure that the specifier has no problems or queries and, more important, to make sure that he calls when the specification is being written.

The Specifier

Unlike most commercial organisations, architectural and engineering practices authorise many people to specify. It may be that different employees have different limits set on their specifying power, but the important fact is that *most can specify to some degree*.

This means that the salesman calling on these firms must be

sure to meet all the employees who are in a position to influence the use of his product, and should regard each of these individual specifiers as a decision maker.

Many specifying organisations are very large, employing several hundred people who are usually divided into teams. The competent salesman should be able to establish which teams are potential users of his equipment and even, perhaps, which members of the team have been made responsible for his particular kind of product.

Whether a salesman starts by seeing the senior executives and working down, or works up from the junior draughtsman, is irrelevant, so long as he meets all the potential specifiers of his company's wares.

The salesman should remember that specifiers are concerned with the choice of many thousands of products and services and, therefore, they have to be constantly reminded of *his* range of products. If he does not do this effectively, they will tend to limit their use of his range of products to the equipment with which they are most familiar. It seems so difficult for the salesman who is constantly meeting the same people to discipline himself to remind clients regularly about the full range of products he is offering, but the fact remains that if he does not do so, some of the products will inevitably be forgotten.

Importance of Trust

The salesman must appreciate that any specifying authority which selects and names his company's equipment is putting its trust in the product, and in the company manufacturing that product. If, for any reason, it does not perform up to expectation, then the specifier's reputation will be affected. *A specifier will guard his reputation jealously.*

When a specifier names a product he is, in effect, publishing the fact that, as an independent expert, he has surveyed the market and selected the equipment as being the best for that particular job. This explains why he is so wary of selecting an unfamiliar product.

To overcome this attitude the salesman has to build up a

relationship which results in the specifier trusting him. The salesman must support the specifier when there are problems, progress orders, deal quickly with complaints, if necessary attend meetings, and accept the responsibility for company mistakes.

A specifying executive once summed up the situation: 'Why is it that when a large contract comes into our office salesmen buzz around us like bees around a honeypot, but if things go wrong you can never contact these salesmen?' He went on with the remark which is the maxim of many buyers: 'The only time I can judge a company is when something goes wrong. Only then can I determine whether they are the kind of company with whom I like to do business.'

The Salesman

The salesman selling to specifying authorities must be patient and methodical. There is often no quick way to secure orders, and in any case, most companies are not looking for one single order but for a continuing stream of contracts. Specifying authorities are to many companies the very lifeblood of their business. In all major projects it is the specifier who calls the tune and decides whether one product or another is used.

The specifier also performs one other very important function which is of great assistance to a company: Every time a company's name is published in a specification that name is read by the trade, and there is no better way of advertising a firm than to have it specified by an independent expert authority.

What then, in simple terms, should be the objective of the salesman calling on the specifying authority? Surely it is this:

> *The salesman's aim should be to persuade every specifying authority in his area to be a salesman for his company.*

15

Territory Planning and Management

Robert Levene, managing director of Tack Research Ltd, is responsible for the various surveys referred to in this book. He is also researching continually into territory planning, to enable salesmen attending our courses to learn the most effective way of covering their ground.

Here are his views on territory planning:

It is obvious that the number, size, and composition of individual sales territories must vary widely from company to company, depending upon differing industrial and commercial contexts. Equally, it is clear that the primary purpose of allocating territories is to establish a basis for the sales director or manager to control and direct the activities of his team.

In every case, the sales executive would rightly expect to be judged by the results he obtains through his team. The ideal criteria could be summarised as the achievement of maximum sales of every product or service, to every suitable outlet—at maximum profit.

Rather less self-evident is the proposition that the industrial salesman can equally appropriately be judged by the same criteria. The difference is purely one of scale. The salesman should be aiming for the same desirable end results from his personal territory which the sales manager sets out to achieve nationally.

The salesman who, in fact, achieved maximum sales of every product, to every suitable outlet at maximum profit, would be proving his ability as his own sales manager. Such a man would be demonstrating his professional skill as a director of sales— for that is what he is—on his own specified territory.

The way each salesman manages his own territory is a very clear indication to senior management of his suitability, or lack of it, for field management responsibilities, with commensurate rewards.

Naturally, the time scale for obtaining orders varies markedly with the industrial product or service concerned. This may involve selling to committees, to specifying authorities, to consultants, and the like. In every case, however, the salesman will expect to be judged by the business which accrues to his company, directly or indirectly, over an appropriate period of time. These results of his efforts, which we may conveniently term his effectiveness, cannot be viewed in isolation. Their real value can only be assessed when related to the costs incurred.

With this fair criterion of cost effectiveness established, it will be useful to consider separately the elements involved in that ratio or relationship.

Firstly we may restrict our cost consideration to the prime direct cost of a salesman. This is simply the gross annual income he receives.

Each salesman who reads these words will know his current figure, which he could express as, 'I earn £X per year'. While the value of X will vary considerably from man to man, the year is the same for everyone.

Yet that constant of 365 days is, in selling terms, a gross overstatement. More realistically it is true to say that most salesmen usually work 5 days a week, so that 52 weeks of 5 days give a starting figure of 260 days. From this there have to be deducted the 8 statutory United Kingdom bank holidays, and, from the resultant 252 days, a typical 3 weeks' holiday would remove another 15 working days. This leaves, at best, 237 days, on the assumption that no days are lost through sickness or other causes. This means that our earlier figure of £X per year has to be divided by 237 (and not by 365) to arrive at the bare daily cost.

Knowing his own annual income, every salesman who reads these words could now write in the margin of this page the bare daily cost to his company of keeping him on his territory. Yet that figure would still be very much below the current reality.

A moment's consideration will show that other fixed and

variable sales costs have also to be taken into account. Apart from the costs of running the company car, or of allowances for his own car, each salesman can include fixed or variable payments for meals, hotels, entertaining, etc. Less immediately obvious are the considerable costs of recruitment, plus subsequent internal and/or external product and sales training. Again, advertising and exhibition costs have to be spread over the sales force, while there are also the vital support costs incurred by field management, indoor technical and other office support staff—not excluding sales management costs.

From this it must be evident that the salesman's bare £X per year gross income is but the base of a sales cost pyramid.

For each salesman, the true value of the total company investment—for that is what it is—is likely to be at least twice the prime cost of the salesman's gross annual income. In fact, the actual figure can be four or more times the basic figure of the salesman's income.

A piece of rapid mental calculation by each salesman reader has doubtless already taken place! Let no salesman feel discouraged or dispirited by the resultant figures. The intention is solely to clarify the range and scale of financial commitment involved when a salesman is recruited, trained, equipped, and supported on his allotted territory.

Assuredly, the senior management of every company will be inescapably aware of the total sales costs of its own operations. All the relevant factors have to be taken into account before a rational price policy can be decided, with the twin aims of being both competitive and profitable.

The essential message is that irrespective of the products or service, any salesman's avoidable weaknesses in territory coverage must involve his company in far from inconsiderable excess costs. Conversely, the salesman who really covers his territory effectively will achieve above-average profitability.

Since higher profitability must benefit both the company and the salesman, due consideration must now be given to factors affecting a salesman's effectiveness. Classic method study principles will assist our careful consideration of this vital aspect.

The first question we could, therefore, ask of any salesman is, *where* do you work? Almost invariably, the reply will be in geographical terms such as, the Midlands, Yorkshire, or in postal terms such as London EC1, 2, 3 or 4.

The convenience of such descriptions should not mask the fact that they are a form of verbal shorthand. No salesman covers a geographical unit in its entirety. Within his defined boundary there are many individuals and groups of particular kinds, in a wide variety of businesses and activities. Effectively, the only ones who count are those with whom or through whom the salesman is, or could be, obtaining business.

Efficient territory management, therefore, calls for careful planning to cover most effectively the relevant types of customers/ specifiers. The specifiers could include such groups as consultant engineers or architects, while the direct customers could be, say, foundries or furniture manufacturers. In all cases the customers and specifiers may be subdivided into actual and potential categories. This means that as a first task, each salesman must have his own customers and prospects listed as fully as possible, both by location and alphabetically. The extent and nature of past company records and of professional, trade or other directories, will affect the ease of obtaining the relevant data, but the more accurate and exhaustive the list, the sounder will be the basis for building business.

The next step is to grade the listed customers and prospects in terms of their actual or potential importance. Typically, there will be a relatively small number of customers who are of major importance and who provide a high percentage of the total territory turnover. Such people we may term the Grade A customers. Second there will be those (Grade B) who are of medium size, and more numerous than Grade A. Further subdivision of customers will vary with the marketing operation and context of the company concerned. This could well lead to two further grades, C and D, the former being small customers who are expanding and the latter those small customers where business is declining.

Each salesman will, or should, know what subdivisions are

valid in his own case, and can make appropriate adjustments to succeeding details. Since we are here concerned with general principles, we shall take as a typical example the four categories A, B, C, and D, and further assume the actual number in each category is A 10, B 20, C 50, and D 60. Whether or not this total of 140 customers produces an inadequate, adequate or excessive work load for one salesman, will depend on many further factors.

First, there is the frequency with which visits need to be made to customers in each category. Second, the length of time justifiably *invested* in sales discussion will also vary with each outlet's actual or potential business value.

At one extreme, one salesman may have one or more major customers who need to be seen weekly, and with whom discussions involve hours rather than minutes. At the other extreme visits to major customers might correctly and safely be made at quarterly intervals, and again, the time of each call could vary markedly in accordance with the product or service under discussion.

In the following continuation of our examples, it will be seen that the frequency of calls varies from monthly to as little as six-monthly on Grade D establishments. Similarly, the time varies from a maximum investment of one and a half hours to a minimum half an hour.

Grade of Customer/Prospect	A (major)	B (medium)	C (small, but expanding)	D (small, but diminishing)
Number	10	20	50	60
Calls p.a.	12	8	4	2
Duration of call	$1\frac{1}{2}$ hr	1 hr	1 hr	$\frac{1}{2}$ hr
Total hours	180	160	200	60

In this notional example the annual time spent on calls totals 600 hours and, as earlier established, there are 237 selling days available annually. In round terms, this points to an average of two and a half hours daily in face-to-face meetings with customers and prospects. Although this figure is close to the average face-to-face time established by many industrial sales forces, we cannot yet form any conclusions about the viability of our imaginary territory of 140 customers and prospects.

Having considered the *who* and *when* factors, these must now be related to the all important consideration of *where* the calls have to be made. For this purpose, appropriate maps are essential. The scale might well vary from six inch to the mile street plans of major towns, to quarter inch maps of largely rural areas with widely dispersed points of call. Whatever the scale, either the map itself or some suitable transparent sheeting placed over it now needs to be marked.

Using plastic markers of varying shapes and colours, flags, pins, or any other suitable indicators, all known customers and prospects can now be physically indicated in their precise locations. The resultant distribution will never be of uniform density. Each salesman will note his own convenient clusters of customers as well as those, major or otherwise, who are relatively remote from other calls. For optimum cost effectiveness, the invariable need is to subdivide the territory so as to provide as far as possible an even work load every day.

It is here that the salesman's personal knowledge of his territory has to be called in aid. His awareness of the local topography, the changing road and other communications, will help determine the most efficient subdivision of the ground and work to be covered. At its simplest, with the territory being covered weekly, the resultant workday breakdown could be as in figure 1(a).

The strength, and also the weakness, of this routine would be that every Monday the salesman would be in the same part of his territory. Were an important customer not available on a given Monday, a prompt special diversion would have to be made later that week, or the visit left until the following Monday.

Further, for the first part of each week the salesman would always be in the eastern part of his territory, invariably moving westwards towards the end of the week. This latter problem

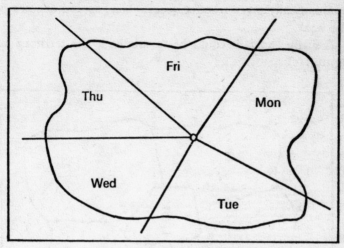

Fig. 1a: Simple weekly cycle

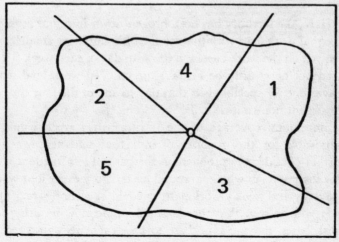

Fig. 1b.

would be reduced by the routine shown in figure 1(b) which automatically gives a better geographical spread of work over the week.

A further variant could be to subdivide the territory as in figure 1(c).

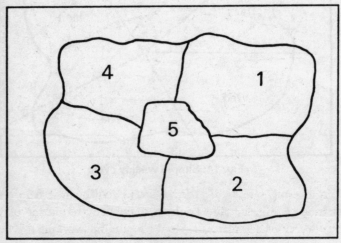

Fig. 1c.

Here, the territory has been broken down into four segments of equal work load with that for the fifth day being smaller, and centred on the work base. On this fifth day of each week (which need not necessarily be Friday) the reduced work load would leave time for special visits that day to any of the four quarters for urgent non-routine calls.

Since total coverage of the territory in a week would be impossible for the majority of industrial salesmen, we must further consider the problem on the basis of less frequent visits. For the salesman who goes round his territory every four weeks, the daily and weekly work pattern could be as in figure 2(a).

It will be seen that the salesman would now be using four work bases, moving from base to base each week in a regular clockwise pattern. Further, within any given week there would be an additional routine order of daily working.

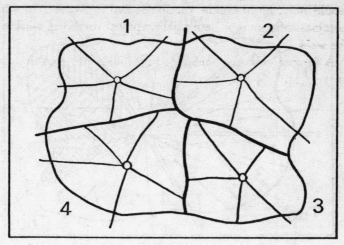

Fig. 2a.

As a result, one, two, or three weeks could elapse before the salesman would be due back in a particular quarter of the territory. Furthermore, he would again be working his way round that particular quarter in the set daily rotation.

The evident limitations of this highly organised but inflexible work pattern mean that, overall size of territory permitting, it could be broken down on a preferable basis. The four-weekly journey would be subdivided into segments on a modular basis, with the individual daily journeys being related to actual cycles of territory coverage. With each sub-segment now containing one day's work, the planned breakdown of a four-weekly rotation would be as represented in Figure 2(b).

Two features of this method will be noted. Firstly, having worked a particular sub segment on the first Monday of the month (Mon 1), the routine automatically brings the salesman into the adjacent sub-segment just a week later (Mon 2). Although still working on a monthly cycle, this means that a call missed on a given Monday could automatically be included for the journey on the following Monday. The detour would be minimal.

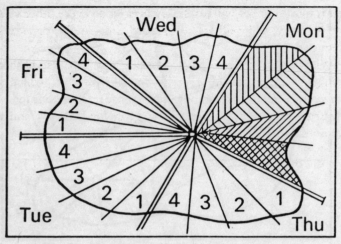

Fig. 2b: Modular working, with daily segments

Secondly, as Figure 2(b) shows, strict clockwise or anti-clockwise order is modified, with advantage. Having returned to his home or hotel base at the end of Mon 1, the planned pattern of visits now means that the next day the salesman will move in the opposite direction to cover sub-segment Tues 1. Similarly, work on Wed 1, Thu 1, and Fri 1 will produce a well-distributed pattern of work. This could be likened to the spacing of the blades on a five-bladed propeller fan.

Unavoidably, whatever plans are made there will be exceptional emergencies which will justify unscheduled departures from orderly working. Nevertheless this does not alter the general value of the method and principles here outlined. For every salesman, the more organised and regular his work pattern, the more effectively he will cover his territory in the most economical fashion. With coverage at optimum efficiency, the results in terms of sales are bound to follow suit.

The varied composition of any day's activities will naturally have to be determined by the relative importance of customers whose premises are in the piece of territory to be covered.

For example, major customers will invariably be visited while less important ones will justifiably be seen on every other visit to the territory, some others every third time round, or even less frequently.

With the make-up of each working day thus established a critically important factor will be the order in which the correctly included customers and prospects are visited. To illustrate this point an example is given in Figure 3 and this assumes a total of seven justified calls.

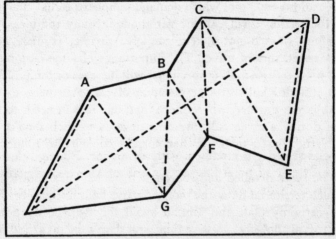

Fig. 3: The 'petal' system

One method would be the so called 'out and home' route, where the first call is made on the most distant customer (D) to be visited that day. Thereafter, calls will be made on E, C, F, B, G, A and finally back to starting point.

Alternatively, the dotted line could be followed in reverse order, with the longest journey from D to base being left to the end of the day. The first call, on the nearest customer, will thus be A, and the dotted line journey will then be G, B, F, C, E and, finally, D.

Obviously, the hours of starting and finishing the first and last calls vary from salesman to salesman, and this major point will be the subject of later comment.

Nevertheless it must be apparent that if the order of visiting were A–B–C–D–E–F–G this peripheral, or so called 'petal' method would be shorter than the alternative criss-cross methods. In essence, the 'petal' system is based on making the mid point of the daily journey the mid point of the calls. The reader can quickly check the advantage of this principle for himself. It merely involves marking a map with an actual day's scheduled calls, and then comparing the dotted line distance with the perimeter journey of the 'petal' method.

An additional point which demands emphasis is that changes on the territory will call for variations in daily routines. No carefully worked out system can give precise, regular, and permanent lines of travel. The importance of some customers and prospects (including specifiers) will increase or diminish so that differing call rates or duration of calls will need to be established. Further, where more than one person needs to be seen during a given call, the time devoted to each should be correctly related to his or her current capacity to influence buying decisions.

The more detailed and thorough the salesman's knowledge of such territorial data, the more effective he is likely to be. He can certainly plan and aim to avoid the twin occupational hazards of allowing excessive time with the wrong man, and not enough time with the right man.

Essentially, the message to the salesman is that the principles already set out will always need to be related to his individual circumstance, and then applied with commonsense flexibility. This general strategy of territory planning will, nevertheless, need to be supported by sound daily tactics if optimum results are to be achieved.

The tactical requirement is to make the most effective use of each day. This means investing as much time as possible in face-to-face discussions and, conversely, minimising the unproductive overhead time. It is in this respect that the salesman's abilities as a manager are fully tested. Unlike the man on the shop floor or in the office, he has to be his own daily manager.

Though no salesman would deliberately set out to be a poor

self-manager, there is ample evidence to show that standards do vary widely, even within a given sales force. Not surprisingly, a frequent underlying weakness is the slow but pernicious drift into habits that can be far more costly than is realised. For example, the loss of an hour's selling time a day may not appear to be a particularly damaging defect. Nevertheless many a reader will already be relating this loss to figures earlier discussed. Since the year is effectively but 237 days, this means in round terms that an hour lost daily adds up to 30 eight-hour days a year. Since the five-day week is virtually standard, this means a loss of six weeks in a year. Put more positively, this equally means that an extra hour per day in face-to-face selling would add an extra six weeks to a salesman's year. Such a desirable objective can only be attained by determined effort.

However, this must follow careful consideration of the actual times at which salesmen make their first and last calls because of, or despite, the distances to be covered. Let it be at once agreed that these times are not solely for the salesman to determine. He can only be seen when his customer is both able and willing to grant an interview.

Equally arguable is the fact that, in any given commercial and industrial context there will be a normal starting time. Yet in every group of customers and prospects there will always be those who begin earlier than most of their kind. Salesmen are no different. Those who are weak self managers and who lack personal discipline will provide themselves with adequate explanations why their first calls should be delayed until an unnecessarily late starting time. This attitude is typified by the all-embracing statement that 'they won't see me until . . .'

Whatever the time thus named there are bound to be some buyers, possibly a minority, who would be ready to interview salesmen at a still earlier hour. The pertinent question for the salesman to ask himself is whether it is he who takes advantage of these opportunities, or whether he permits his competitor to get in ahead of him.

Here let it be clearly stated that there can be no set time at which every salesman should be making his first call. This must be determined by the work pattern of those to be visited. Overall, the facts are as set out in the following table (extracted from the latest edition of the Tack Survey, *Buyers' Views on Salesmen*). The figures relate to a sample of 1,040 buyers, in the widest generic sense of that term, who were properly classified not only by personal function, but also by geographical location, and by the nature of their business or activity.

Table 1   Buyers' starting times/earliest interview times

| | Percentage of buyers now | |
Time	Starting work	Able to see first salesman
hours	%	%
0600*	1·3	
0630	1·7	
0700	1·7	
0730	2·9	
0800	7·5	1·5
0830	23·2	4·7
0900	44·7	24·5
0930	15·1	26·4
1000	1·9	30·5
1030		7·4
1100		3·5
1130†		1·5
Totals	100·0	100·0

* Or earlier
† Or later

While three in ten would not see salesmen before ten a.m. over half began at nine-thirty, or nine o'clock. Significantly, almost one in twenty began at eight-thirty.

In the light of these facts plus his own knowledge of his industry, his territory, and his customers, each salesman would surely be wise to consider whether it would be possible to find each day just one customer who could be visited one hour earlier than the present earliest. The result would be the equivalent of six weeks' extra selling time. Even half an hour a day would result in three weeks extra, which would be a worthwhile objective for any salesman determined to improve his performance through efficient self-management.

Such self-management would also productively aid any salesman whose calls are largely, if not exclusively, made by appointment. With the need for planning clearly in mind he would avoid asking, 'When would you like me to call?' Given such an open question the likely telephone response from the buyer would be mid-morning or mid-afternoon times, typically ten-thirty or eleven, and fourteen-thirty or fifteen hundred hours.

Prior consideration before telephoning would enable the time-conscious salesman to work out his most efficient route for the calls due on the day concerned. Study of his territory might indicate that the first three calls at X, Y, and Z, would best be made in the order Z, X, and Y, with, if possible, the additional call on Q being made first. If this were the case the telephone call to Q would make use of the invaluable alternative close to fix the time in such terms as, 'Would eight-thirty or nine o'clock be better for you, Mr Smith?'

Although such a suggestion will often lead to an appointment at one or other of the suggested times, this will not invariably be so. If the buyer were to respond that his earliest interview time was nine-thirty, then that would at once be accepted by the salesman who knows that no one else could have secured an earlier interview.

An additional problem which has to be faced is that even the most carefully planned schedules get out of hand. When an interview ends half-way through an allotted hour the decision about time utilisation will properly depend on the salesman's judgement and territorial knowledge. In some instances the half hour of 'spare' time could profitably be used to make full or preliminary fact finding calls on near-by prospects.

Where the distances involved prevent such intermediate visits then, with diary in hand, the salesman's time might well be devoted to the telephone. The purpose would be to make convenient fresh appointments for following days or weeks, dependent on the relevant lead time.

Alternatively, with a commendable degree of flexibility and initiative, the salesman could telephone the secretary of the man with whom the next appointment had previously been fixed. His courteous and helpful suggestions could well be expressed in terms along the following lines:

> 'Miss Thompson, my name is George White and as you know I am due to see Mr Smith at eleven-thirty this morning. Now if it would help him or be preferable, I could be with you by eleven instead. Could you please tell me what time Mr Smith would prefer?'

Often, the secretary will confirm either immediately or after a brief word with her Mr Smith, that the earlier time will be perfectly suitable. Occasionally the alteration may fit in with the interviewer's day more easily than the original time. In any case, the polite consideration will be appreciated, while it is not unknown in such circumstances for the buyer to express his regret if he is unable to alter the original timing.

By the same token, when any interview demands and warrants greater time than was initially allotted when planning the day's work, this need cause no panic. A polite request to be allowed a moment to telephone will invariably be granted, and the salesman can then explain suitably to whoever is next expecting him. The next interview time can often then be set back, with the buyer's agreement. This has the additional merit of avoiding driving under great tension in a dangerous attempt to make good excess time devoted to the preceding interview.

Thus it is that, with an early start and using an appointment system flexibly, the organised salesman can increase his real selling time each day. Such a man will need no urging to give as much consideration to his finishing times as to his time of starting work.

Again, the full spread of selling opportunities is grasped by some salesmen, but artificially restricted by others. The facts, resulting from research, are set out in Table 2 which has been extracted from the Tack survey earlier mentioned.

Table 2   Buyers' last interview times/finishing times

| Time | Percentage of buyers now | |
	Able to see last salesman	Finishing work
hours	%	%
1300*	4·3	
—	—	—
1500	3·3	
1530	4·3	
1600	26·4	
1630	21·3	2·3
1700	22·4	11·6
1730	8·4	27·4
1800	6·9	29·6
1830†	2·7	11·6
1900		8·7
1930		3·1
2000		2·2
2030†		3·5
Totals	100·0	100·0

* Or earlier
† Or later

While over one in four buyers started their last interview not later than 1600 hours, over one in five could be interviewed at 1630, and slightly more at 1700. The opportunities still available at 1730 and 1800 will not be ignored by any salesman determined to be a really effective self-manager.

Again, it must be made abundantly clear that it is not possible for every salesman to start his final interview at 1800 every day. Yet, in every salesman's life there occur those unhappy days which produce nothing but complaints or queries. It is then that the insidious temptation to stop work early can become irresistible. Conscience is saved with the rationalisation that more harm than good will be achieved by making any more calls on such a day. The one sure outcome of such a decision is that the salesman denies himself the possibility of redressing the unfavourable balance of his unwisely curtailed day.

Many a salesman faced with such a situation has resolutely gone on to make an extra call with a clear sales objective in mind. When such a call proves productive the salesman's creative satisfaction and sense of personal achievement are his own well-deserved rewards. He needs no conversion to the principle that the business he achieves is directly related to the face-to-face time spent with customers.

The average time thus spent daily is two hours, twenty minutes. The salesman who has carefully studied the pages of this book will have been provided with abundant food for thought. Properly digested and put into daily practice, his enhanced professional skills will assuredly result in sales interviews of a higher quality.

Admirable as such an aim must be it will not, on its own, enable him to achieve his full potential. For the ultimate fulfilment of his potential as a personal sales manager he must be prepared to study, and consider quantity as well as quality.

Armed with his own watch and a determination to be totally honest with himself, he need work only one week bearing fully in mind the thoughts and guidance presented in these pages. A man doing this can quickly discover whether his total daily face-to-face time is above or below the average. More pertinently, it will help him in his self-critical task of deciding whether, and how, he can improve his sales performance.

When he does that—and inevitably progresses as a result—he will deserve his success.

16

The Professional Salesman

Most of us involved in marketing refer, on occasion, to the *professional salesman*. What does this mean?

The three learned professions are divinity, medicine, and law, but in modern dictionaries there is an additional definition of a profession: *a calling, vocation, or occupation involving high educational or technical qualifications*. This definition now applies not only to accountants, architects, and teachers, but also to actors, authors, and salesmen. But unlike factory, office, or farm workers with incomes related to hours, productivity, or the cost of living, the actor, sportsman, or author is directly rewarded according to his efforts and ability. When someone refers to an actor as being a *true professional*, the inference is that even if temperamental, he still listens carefully and heeds the advice of his director, is punctual at rehearsals, and gives of his best even when worried or ill. When we refer to a footballer as a *true professional*, we mean someone who is always *trying*, and who doesn't squirm on the ground after receiving a slight knock— and who is not forever complaining of bad management, unfair crowds, or that his colleagues let him down.

Although industrial selling is not a profession, in the sense that medicine, law, or accountancy are professions, it does meet the modern dictionary definition of a profession—a *calling, vocation, or occupation involving high educational or technical qualifications*. The industrial salesman, more often than not, has technical qualifications of a high standard. Also like the doctor, dentist, author, actor, and sportsman, the income of the industrial salesman is nearly always related directly to his personal efforts. This applies even when there is no commission element.

Again referring to the dictionary we find another definition of professional: *of or pertaining to a profession as opposed to an amateur*. The inference, therefore, when a film producer says of a film star that he is a *true professional*, or a cricket captain says of a bowler, ever eager for work, that he is a *real professional*, is that some actors or cricketers are amateurs. Many industrial salesmen are *true professionals*, while others can fairly be termed amateurs.

Professional Standards

What are the qualifications necessary for a man to become a *true professional*?

An article in the magazine *Salesmanship* listed the qualities of the ideal salesman:

> honesty
> empathy
> 'stickability'
> understanding of human relations
> command of language
> persuasiveness
> ability to communicate
> ambition
> tact
> initiative
> 'self-starter'
> integrity
> warm, friendly personality
> even temperament
> willingness to learn
> sense of humour
> courage
> good health
> hard worker

Phew! If I met anyone with all those attributes I should expect to see a halo round his head. Sales executives, in particular, when advertising for salesmen, are apt to stress such qualities as persistence, self-starter, or hard worker. But it's doubtful whether those sales executives have ever interviewed a salesman who did not believe that he was persistent, a hard worker, and needed no supervision. We all believe that we have many attributes which, in reality, we don't possess.

It is worth the effort of analysing ourselves now and again, because this allows us to attempt to eradicate any selling faults we may have. Some, we can overcome completely. Others are in-built and may be mastered one day only to plague us again later. But none of us could live up to the title *ideal salesman* as defined by *Salesmanship*. We couldn't have all of the qualities all of the time and still remain human. The professional salesman is not some superman who works from 7 a.m. until 7 p.m. every day, doesn't waste time over lunch, smiles when things go wrong, and always agrees with the directives of his sales manager or managing director. He is an individual who can sometimes be really awkward. He will always fight for what he believes to be right, but unlike the amateur, he only stands firm when he has analysed the total situation. He neither bends with the wind nor argues when he knows he is in the wrong. His main characteristics are:

> enthusiasm
> ability to absorb knowledge
> willingness to learn and develop selling skills
> willingness to accept and apply new ideas.

You may well ask: Surely honesty and integrity are all important? Of course they are, but these virtues apply to everyone in every walk of life. A man should not claim to be honest and expect to be congratulated. It is a minus sign if a person is dishonest and lacks integrity, it is not a plus if he possesses what the law and general decency demand of everyone.

'That is true,' a sales manager might say—and then add, 'but you must agree that a salesman should be a self-starter, persistent, and a hard worker. So it's as well to pinpoint these assets.'

We all vary from time to time in the efforts we make to succeed. We cannot be 100% persuasive at every call; we cannot always leave our house or flat brimful of excitement at the thought of making the first call. Even in sport a man cannot maintain the same high standards of training or performance every day. The true professional salesman, more often than not, is persistent—is a hard worker—is dedicated to the work which gives him so much enjoyment. Why? Because of his enthusiasm.

Enthusiasm enhances every quality a salesman needs to be a professional. However, enthusiasm is not the sole prerogative of the extrovert. Industrial salesmen are sometimes quiet, unobtrusive men, but they still possess that 'fire in the belly' which urges them on to do better. When a man is enthusiastic, all the other qualities which lead a salesman to success fall into place. The enthusiast always works hard, for the simple reason that he enjoys his work.

Most salesmen can be driven for a *short* period to work harder by an incentive—a competition prize, or a bonus offer. Others increase sales on receiving a warning from head office; and there is always the man who reserves his best effort for the occasional visits of his sales manager or field sales manager. The enthusiast will have his off days, like everyone else; but they are scattered far apart. He is the man who wants to work hard because he enjoys the challenge always implicit in selling. The enthusiast is a self-starter, and because of his enthusiasm for his product and his company, he will always have the ability to persuade and to change minds.

WILLINGNESS TO ABSORB KNOWLEDGE

Here are some figures from a Tack Survey, *Buyers' Views on Salesmen*:

    1,040 buyers responded to a questionnaire.

    Question No. 5 was:

    Generally speaking do you find that salesmen's knowledge of their own products and prices is . . . VERY GOOD

                          GOOD

                          FAIR

                          INADEQUATE

                          POOR

Here is a summary of the answers:

VERY GOOD	176	17%
GOOD	497	48%
FAIR	312	30%
INADEQUATE	49	4%
POOR	6	1%
	1,040	100%

Surely, if every salesman were a professional, under the heading *very good* the figure would be at least 50%? And is *good* good enough?

Check these figures again, and you will see that 35%—that is one in three of every salesman calling on buyers—lack complete product knowledge.

This indicates that by the law of averages, 35% of the salesmen reading this book have inadequate product knowledge. A salutary thought.

Poor product knowledge could be due to lack of training, lack of the ability to assimilate knowledge, or lack of interest. Many companies give first-class product training in courses varying from one week to several months. The average (again taken from a Tack Survey) is three weeks. However, approximately only one company in five, during product training, gives a series of tests to discover whether or not the knowledge is being assimilated.

Only one company in thirty holds meetings during the year when further tests are given to ensure that salesmen have acquired product knowledge sent to them by letters, bulletins, literature, brochures, instruction sheets, etc.

More often than not the onus is on the salesman to perfect his product knowledge. The professional salesman avidly reads every item of news from head office, while men who are less enthusiastic sometimes complain of the mass of bumph they receive, and file away the memoranda, leaflets, and price lists, meaning to study them at a later date. There rarely is a later date. Having glanced at them, they make themselves believe that they are well informed.

The professional salesman never uses the excuse, *the company never tells us anything*. He doesn't always wait to be told—he asks, demands, badgers, if necessary, to get information which he believes will help him to get business.

Knowledge of Customers

The professional salesman always has a good understanding of his customers' business ramifications, which enables him to build a sales presentation based on their needs and to give them the best possible advice.

He likes to know their:

    quality requirements
    manufacturing processes
    inventory policies
    tendering procedures
    share of the market
    competition
    development plans
    export markets
    buying procedures
    problems to be solved
    standards of testing.

It would be very useful if we all had good memories. Most people are apt to forget a man's name and his background within a day or so of meeting him. This is due to a lack of a real interest in that person.

But a salesman must remember everything about his customers—not only the names of decision influencers, but their interests and hobbies, likes and dislikes. The problem is often not so much a bad memory as half listening. If we concentrate on what the other person is saying we are more likely to remember what he says.

Knowledge of Company Policy

Is there a salesman who has not had a day ruined by a letter received from head office which either condemns, reprimands, or refuses to co-operate? Is there a salesman who has never rushed out of a customer's premises to the nearest telephone to blast head office for inefficiency?

Those at head office do, of course, make mistakes and, on occasion, salesmen's customers are let down. This is because business is run by human beings, and human beings invariably make a percentage of mistakes, quite apart from errors of judgment.

Often, however, when a salesman loses good selling time through aggravation or making telephone calls to demand an explanation, he could save himself expending so much nervous energy by reminding himself of company policy.

When orders are at stake, or when a customer complains, company policy recedes into the background of the salesman's mind. He forgets the strict credit measures laid down by credit control, and offers a customer special credit facilities. He overlooks the rules about discounts, and becomes furious when a customer complains that a discount promised has not been allowed. Salesmen do so often promise special conditions, or guarantee quick deliveries. Sales managers can instruct that nothing can be delivered under three months—that there can be no deviation from a specification—that no goods can be held in stock on behalf of a customer. But salesmen still go against such rules. Yet the life of a salesman can be made so much easier if he knows, understands, and carries out his company's policies.

Knowledge of Competitors

Against all odds, Sunderland beat Leeds in the 1973 Cup Final. Bob Stokoe, manager of Sunderland said, at that time, 'There are many reasons why we beat Arsenal in the semi-final and Leeds to win the Cup. We had marvellous support from our fans, we had splendid team spirit, and outstanding players but also we *knew the opposition*. We studied both Arsenal and Leeds, and knew what we could expect. Our plan was to counter their moves most of the time, while using the advantages we have and the skills of our individual players.'

Good common sense that! In business also, it pays to study

the competition carefully, not for the purpose of directly attacking a competitor—that never wins orders—but to enable a salesman to stress the advantages of his product in those areas in which his competitors are weakest.

Any information you can honestly obtain about your competitors' products or services will help you to sell more successfully, but never take notice of the rumours which spread so quickly in the world of selling. From time to time sales managers hear this kind of statement about competitors:

> 'They are almost giving away their products to keep their factory busy.'
>
> 'They want to knock out competition—they've cut their prices to the bone.'
>
> 'They are not now charging for deliveries—that is what is really affecting me.'
>
> 'Did you know they've doubled their consultancy staff?'
>
> 'They're willing to provide equipment for trial purposes.'
>
> 'They're even willing to give twelve months' credit to get orders.'

These are the kind of rumours which send a salesman rushing to the telephone to explain to his sales manager why he can't get business against his competitors. Most rumours, if checked, will be found to be untrue.

A salesman's knowledge of his competitors should be based on the claims made by them in their brochures and in their advertising, and on what reliable customers say about them (always remembering that buyers will hint at special concessions they receive from competitors only to obtain an extra concession from you). On many occasions, too, a salesman can examine his competitors' products, because they are in offices or factories for everyone to see.

The professional salesman knows almost as much about his competitors' products as they do themselves.

THE RIGHT MENTAL ATTITUDE

The world is full of frustrated salesmen—men who believe that they are held back because of lack of understanding, lack of appreciation, lack of the ability of head office management.

'Why can't the sales manager understand,' says one salesman 'that I'm different. I'm not the kind of man who can work to a set of rules. I like going my own way.'

Someone once said that every salesman, like every sportsman, should repeat to himself every day: *The only man who need not keep to any rules is the genius, and just in case I am not a genius, I'd better keep to them.*

Other salesmen say, 'Why don't they appreciate that I'm a man with ideas? I keep telling them how they can increase their business. All they have to do is:

'Give me an assistant.'

or

'Promote me.'

or

'Give me more territory.'

or

'Increase my expenses so that I can entertain at a higher level.'

or

'Give me a bigger car.'

A third category of salesmen are more direct in their criticism:

'They haven't any ability at head office.'

'They never get quotations out on time.'

'They can never give a quick decision.'

'They don't know how to write a letter.'

'They don't understand the first thing about selling.'

'Why do they keep sending me bumph?'

There is usually common sense behind the instructions, rules, and advice sent out by head office, but understandably, the salesman and his sales director sometimes have different outlooks. The salesman is deeply concerned with his customers' interests and in obtaining new orders. The sales director or sales manager has a similar concern, but he is also closely involved with company policy, budget control, forecasts, capital expenditure, finance, and servicing. The sales director, therefore, has many factors to consider when demands are made upon him by salesmen or area managers.

The giving of special credit to one customer could lead to extended credit to others, and affect the company cash flow.

This does not mean that management is always right. In some companies, management is way behind the times in marketing expertise, and does not give the right backing to its salesmen. But we still live in a free country and no salesman need stay with such a company.

Optimist or Pessimist

A dictionary definition of an optimist is a *person with a disposition to take a bright, hopeful view of things*, while that of the pessimist is *one who believes that everything is tending to the worst*. Very few industrial salesmen are optimistic all the time, and many less are pessimistic most of the time, but most amateur salesmen are neither completely optimistic nor completely pessimistic—they are *up-and-downers*. To them, there is no such thing as the Law of Averages which, for a salesman, means that, with hard work and an ever-improving sales presentation, sales targets will be met in spite of some blank days or weeks. To the *up-and-downer* when an order is lost ('Our prices are ridiculously high and they haven't forgotten we let them down once before!') the future is bleak indeed. But when a big order is confirmed there is sunshine everywhere. Plans are made for summer holidays, a new suit may be purchased, and promotion is only just round the corner.

The professional salesman is never foolishly optimistic. He knows that the *everything will be all right on the day* belief is fatuous, unless backed by the sort of effort which makes things right on the day; but the amateur optimist believes all the buyer tells him.

'It's what we need. When you have the prototype, let me see it.'

'You have a splendid idea there—I'll certainly put it before the board.'

'Just leave the quotation with me and I'll let you know. You need not worry about it.'

They will all be orders claims the optimistic amateur, still not realising that there is a vast difference between a buyer's promises when he is not in a position to buy and his decisions when in a buying situation.

The professional salesman tries to keep a balanced viewpoint. He is an optimist most of the time, a pessimist occasionally, and very rarely an *up-and-downer*. He is so confident of his product and in his own ability that he is not concerned with fearful newspaper headlines, 'a shocking trading month', 'exports drastically down', 'imports getting out of hand', or the predictions of disaster made regularly by bankers, brokers, and financiers. He is concerned only with doing his job right, irrespective of trading conditions. Like everyone else, he will be affected by booms, recessions, and credit squeezes, but he will still get more than his share of the business—not because he is a selling genius, but because he always has the right mental attitude to his work, to his customers, and to his company.

HUMAN RELATIONS

It is extremely difficult to be objective when emotions come into play. If we dislike someone intensely, then when we condemn that person for meanness, untruthfulness, or back stabbing, we are apt to believe that we are being objective when, in fact, we are being motivated mainly by emotional rather than rational thinking.

So often it has been said that we cannot change ourselves. If that were so there would be little purpose in this book, and there would be little use in asking ourselves the question: *Does it apply to me?* when considering aspects of salesmanship.

The majority of people change by associating with others—by learning from life—by environment or by marriage. Psychologists tell us there are many other factors. Revolutionaries at university ten or fifteen years ago are now doctors, lawyers, technicians, engineers, who may not appreciate at all the views of the present-day younger generation.

We can all change our personalities, manners, diets, habits, if we have the will to do so. There are dozens of different facets to the successful conclusion of a negotiation, but the most over-looked is the rapport between the salesman, the buyer, and all those who can influence an order.

We don't have to be psychologists to know what people like or dislike in others. We only have to think of our own reactions to friends, relations, and business associates. Are we always logical in our patterns of behaviour? For example, it is quite illogical for us to take an instant dislike to a person. That man (or woman) can have a heart of gold and spend a lifetime help-ing charities, be sincere and upright in his everyday life. Yet, for some emotional reason, after a five-second glance we decide that we don't really like him. Why? What did he do? Talk too much? Dress too well? Smile insincerely? Swear? Have an effeminate manner?

If we are tidy we do not look kindly upon untidy people. If we are untidy we talk about our houses being 'lived in' and we object to people who are everlastingly emptying ashtrays or straightening cushions. We can please or displease someone by our personal habits, and in the same way we can please or antag-onise a buyer by our idiosyncrasies. The problem is to recog-nise them in ourselves, so that we can set about eradicating them.

For example, few people like anyone to breathe close to their face during a conversation. If we know such a person we avoid him—but do we always keep our distance when speaking to others?

All this means that a professional salesman is conscious that his attitudes, mannerisms, personality, can have a good or a bad effect on buyers. He will check on himself while reading this chapter. Continually, he will ask himself the question: *Does it apply to me?*

The Tack Survey *Buyers' Views on Salesmen* pinpoints some factors in the relationship between buyers and salesmen.

Here is another extract from that survey:

Salesmen's appearance

Whether or not the salesman sees himself as his company's ambassador, his outward appearance is seen by all those on whom he calls. His personal acceptability to a particular buyer can be influenced by a number of elements of his personal appearance. We, therefore, included the following open question: 'Are there any aspects of the salesman's appearance about which you wish to make comment—favourable or unfavourable?' Here is a summary of the answers:

Appearance not important	2%
Prefer neatness	29%
Salesmen mostly well dressed	15%
Salesmen mostly badly dressed	1%
Objections to salesmen's shoes, linen, hairstyles, hands, etc.	20%
Views not expressed	33%
	100%

And here are some comments from buyers answering this section of the survey:

Because people buy from people and not from organisations, other things being equal, a buyer will give an order to the most presentable of two salesmen.

(Buyer—*Business Machine Manufacturers*)

The neatly turned out man always gives a good impression and puts himself 'one up' at once. The opposite type goes 'one down'.

(Managing Director—*Flour Millers*)

A salesman's appearance should be in line with the type of customer he is dealing with.

(Director—*Polish Manufacturer*)

If he is not neat, clean, and efficient, I don't think the company he represents can be.

(Factory Manager—*Fibre Board Manufacturer*)

I am impressed by a tidy salesman, and generally, he will present his facts in a tidy manner.

(Managing Director—*Oil Refinery*)

Condition of hands and fingernails, and cleanliness of shirt collar and tie seem to make the most significant impression on me.

(Chief Engineer—*Television Contractors*)

A mistake commonly made by technical salesmen is summed up in these words: *We're different from other salesmen. The buyers we call upon, engineers and works directors, are concerned only with what my company have to offer, not with my appearance.*

The Tack Survey proves the contrary. While some buyers may not care about a salesman's appearance, others do. The salesman cannot, therefore, take the risk of antagonising those who do—the majority.

The Greeting Handshake

It is doubtful if a salesman will ever lose an order through a handshake, but the question often asked at our courses is: *Should I always offer to shake hands with the buyer?*

The fact that the question is asked even by experienced salesmen highlights the care with which so many salesmen consider every aspect of their job.

The Tack Survey also covers this subject. Here is an extract:

Handshaking

At the beginning and/or end of any sales interview, the salesman might offer his hand to the buyer as a formal or routine gesture, as an intended courtesy, or as a more meaningful expression of true regard or friendship.

Whatever the salesman's intention when proffering his hand, the buyer could react favourably or otherwise.

In order to report how buyers felt about the subject we asked them two linked questions as follows:

Do you shake hands with *all* ☐ salesmen?

              most ☐

              few ☐

              none ☐

Have you any special views on this question?

(a) *General reactions*

The answers to the first question given by every member of the sample, may be summarised thus:

Handshaking

Buyers who shook hands with	Percentage of buyers %
all salesmen	44
most salesmen	37
few salesmen	17
no salesmen	2
Total	100

(b) *Detailed views*

Additional comments were entered by a 40% cross-section of the sample. Here are examples:

I see little point in shaking hands with people I see at regular intervals.

(Joint manager—*Wool Spinners*)

Handshaking is a very friendly gesture, which should be reserved for friends who, indeed, could be salesmen.

(Group managing director—*Quarriers*)

(c) *Disliked handshakes*

Rather more than one in three of those buyers who commented in any way on handshaking made reference to one or more personal feeling of distaste!

These, in order of frequency of mention, were as set out in Table 13.

Here are some comments from buyers:

Dislike the too-hearty handshake which seems insincere and part of the sales routine.

(Personnel director—*Manufacturing Confectioners*)

The weak handshake gives no confidence, and the prolonged handshake annoys me.

(Director—*Printers*)

Table 13

Types of handshakes

Type of handshake	Referred to by percentage of informants
Wet, clammy, cold or fishy	26
Limp	22
Masonic	21
Crushing	12
Pumping	10
Gushing	9
Total	100%

Summary

Although in the main, buyers like or expect to shake hands with salesmen, particularly at a first meeting, it would be wise for the salesman to allow the first movement to come from the buyer.

Smoking

Should the salesman smoke when with a buyer, if the buyer is a non-smoker? Should a non-smoker carry cigarettes with him?

These are questions continually asked, and here is an extract on this subject from the Tack Survey:

Smoking

Each member of the sample was first asked to state whether he or she was a smoker. Next, the following associated questions were put to the respondents:

Do you like ☐ *or dislike* ☐ *a salesman offering you a cigarette?*

Any additional views on salesmen smoking?

Likes, dislikes, and/or comments on salesmen smoking	By percentage of buyers who did not smoke	smoked	Totals
Offer of cigarette:			
liked	3	14	17
liked and commented upon	4	13	17
	7	27	34
disliked	4	5	9
disliked and commented on	10	10	20
	14	15	29
commented on only	14	7	21
no preference or comment	8	8	16
Totals	43	57	100

Though the majority, 57% of buyers, smoke, more than one in four of this group dislike the offer of a cigarette from a salesman.

Here are some comments:

A salesman ought not to smoke in the office of a customer who doesn't smoke.

(Director—*Industrial Consultants*)

As I don't smoke, I think it discourteous if a salesman, knowing this, does so in my office.

(Personnel manager—*Earth Moving Machinery*)

If a salesman doesn't smoke, then I object strongly to being offered a cigarette by him.

(Senior buyer—*Civil Engineering Contractors*)

No objection, providing he doesn't speak with a cigarette in his mouth, or blow smoke in my face.

(Technical supplies officer—*County Council*)

When I decline, I object if the salesman at once asks, 'Do you mind if I do?'

(Managing director—*General Brass Founders*)

Many salesmen immediately offer cigarettes upon introduction or meeting. This I consider a bad ploy, as my acceptance would appear to commit me to a ten-minute interview.

(Quality control manager—*Steel Stockholders*)

Summary

In order to minimise the risk of offence, it is clear that salesmen who do not smoke should not themselves offer a cigarette. The wise salesman would refrain from smoking if he saw that his buyer was not, himself, going to smoke. As a general principle for playing safe, the smoking maxim for salesmen would appear to be: *If in doubt, don't.*

Mannerisms

Public speakers know that however carefully they have prepared a speech and researched their subject, the importance of their points can be lost through mannerisms which jar on the audience. When watching a television interview we are all, on occasion, irritated by the politician who continually plays with a pipe or a button on his jacket, or who keeps straightening his tie. Others constantly waggle a finger or smooth a chin.

Do we irritate others with our mannerisms? Buyers emphasise that mannerisms can cause loss of concentration, and may even result in an interview being cut short.

Check if any of these mannerisms could apply to you:

    playing with a cigarette lighter

    holding a handkerchief in your hand

    drumming with finger tips on chair arm, desk or table

    pushing some object around on the buyer's desk or table

    tilting your chair

  looking at the ceiling, floor, or some object behind the
  buyer's head
  repetition of words or clichés—sort of, O.K., I must
  emphasise, maybe, by and large, as of now, at this moment
  in time, according to our records, in this day and age

Try this test: After checking the list, get the opinion of a
relative or friend. You might find there is a difference between
your knowledge of yourself and how others see you.

Mannerisms which include the inability to look at a buyer
are due either to long-formed habits, or nervousness. Habits,
although difficult to cure, can be cured and the effort must be
made. Constant reminders by friends and family do help (but
are very hard to accept). Nervousness can be overcome by
giving much greater thought to product knowledge, and by
learning to relax.

PERSONALITY

Is there one selling personality? Highly doubtful! Here is an
extract from a dictionary definition of *personality*:
  *The sum of qualities and characteristics which constitute individuals
  —a distinct personal character.*

Possibly most laymen would claim that the man with a selling
personality does have a distinct personality. They picture the
brash salesman they have read about in books and seen on films.
There are many brash salesmen in real life, but they are rarely
successful. There are, of course, highly successful professional
salesmen who are ebullient, have cheerful voices and strong
faces—but that is usually only one side of their characters. They
are accepted by buyers because they are known to be thoroughly
reliable and good ambassadors of their company. They are
not overpowering men whose presence makes a buyer feel
inferior.

There are many professional salesmen with quiet and reserved
personalities. Others could be mistaken for bank managers or
accountants, being so meticulous and transparently honest.

There is not one selling personality, but we do know that

buyers react well to some men, and not to others. Many a salesman has said, 'I didn't get the order because my face didn't fit.' This is another way of saying, 'My personality was not right for that occasion.'

But if a personality is not right for one occasion it is hardly likely that it is any better for others. Such a salesman is always destined to remain average. Men in this category are often too satisfied with the way they are, and make no attempt to eradicate any weaknesses in their personalities which might consciously or subconsciously antagonise a buyer.

What kind of personality does a buyer like in a salesman? Strong? Intense? Agreeable? Dignified? Dynamic? Serene? Vital?

It doesn't really matter what preference he has. The professional salesman knows that his face will always 'fit' because he knows something of human relations. He knows what traits in some salesmen always makes them welcome, while other salesmen receive a message from a secretary, 'I'm sorry, he's too busy to see you today.'

Man is made of many parts, and each part shapes the framework of his main personality. Many small ingredients go into the building of the sales personality. Once these are fixed, a man's personality *can* still change for the better, and personalities do change. An accident can transform a man of happy disposition into a morose, bitter introvert. Marriage can most certainly change a man's personality. The psychologist, William James, said: *The greatest discovery of my generation is that human beings can alter their lives by altering their attitude of mind.*

How can the mind of a salesman be changed so that the change is reflected in his personality? Quite easily—by developing the right mental attitude, and by studying human relations.

Successful industrial salesmen must have four personalities that combine into one. They must have a cheerful personality, a strong personality, a kindly personality, and a sincere personality. Linked together, they form the *selling personality*.

THE CHEERFUL PERSONALITY

Nobody likes the company of miserable or depressing people—least of all buyers. Most of us have troubles enough of our own without being forced to listen to the ills and misfortunes of comparative strangers. Even members of a family do not take kindly to listening to their sister or brother or parents describing in detail their operations, or lecturing them on the decadence of modern society. So why should customers want to listen to similar talk from salesmen?

Too many people are depressing. Why should a customer be expected to be absorbed by the illnesses of salesmen or their families; or by the gruesome accident a salesman has just witnessed; the depth of the snow outside his house; the rapid spread of an influenza epidemic; his fibrositis, rheumatism or migraine headaches; his children's complaints, or his problems with relatives? The list is lengthy. Of course some gloomy people relish sadness and misfortune, so that they, in turn, can elaborate on their own complaints. Most of us, however, prefer cheerfulness to dejection, laughter to tears.

A STRONG PERSONALITY

Strength comes to a salesman from confidence in his ability, and from the knowledge that he can answer every question about his product that a buyer can raise; from knowing that orders will not be lost by his refusal to agree to any unfair demands of buyers.

A buyer, meeting a salesman who is unsure of himself, will weaken him still more. Some instinct tells a buyer which salesmen he can dictate to—and which one he must respect.

Today we read about the uncommitted. A salesman can never be a member of that fraternity. He is committed hook, line, and sinker, to his company and its products or services.

Admit your Mistakes
The weak man is reluctant to admit that he has made a mistake,

and will never apologise when proved wrong, preferring to try and justify his error. Weak salesmen misinterpret the meaning of strength. Some believe it implies toughness, bluntness and being loud-mouthed, but most strong people have no need for displays of this kind. The man who believes that he never makes mistakes cannot be helped. Strangely, he is always the first to say, 'When I am in the wrong I am the first to admit it.' Unfortunately, he never thinks he *is* in the wrong. Any man who learns to admit mistakes can give himself a happier life, and improve his salesmanship.

Ask Advice

How do you react when someone asks your advice? You may have been consulted about fishing tackle, a stamp collection, gardening, *or* salesmanship. Doesn't it give you rather a warm glow—a feeling of well-being and self importance? That is quite normal.

If most people are pleased to give advice, why is their help not sought more often?

Too many take it as a sign of weakness to seek advice—but it is strength, not weakness, to ask the advice of someone competent to give it.

The tycoons of industry would not make a decision without conferring with eminent lawyers, accountants, financiers, scientists, or doctors. Many a small trader relies on his own judgement, and then complains of his bad luck.

A buyer will warm to a salesman who genuinely needs his advice. You always gain strength by having the courage to ask advice from others.

A FRIENDLY PERSONALITY

If a salesman is met with cordiality by everyone, from the commissionaire to the managing director, then he has a friendly personality, and this is not acquired by sycophancy or flattery. A friendly personality does not mean switching on the charm, or being ingratiating. It is a personality that radiates warmth and sincerity.

When the salesman wins the esteem and friendship of the buyer, selling becomes so much easier.

Don't be funny

You don't win friends by being known as a *funny man*. Except, maybe, after a few drinks in a pub, few people appreciate a string of funny stories. One is enough. Others in the gathering are too intent on telling their own favourite anecdotes.

Very few top businessmen tell story after story. It is the lesser men, eager to attract attention to themselves who say, 'Have you heard this one?' It is their one chance, if only for a few fleeting seconds, to capture the limelight, but the more stories a man tells, the more boring he becomes.

Television presents the cream of the world's comedians, men who devote their lives to making others laugh, and who have highly paid script writers to feed them with matter and patter. Even so, seven out of ten of their stories fall flat. Some hardly raise a ripple of laughter. Yet many men—especially salesmen— consider they are good at telling funny stories. They have only to remember how they feel about the stories told to them, to appreciate how theirs are received.

Take no notice of the laughter after one of your stories. It is often forced, and unreal. Only the exceptional story told by the exceptional story-teller is worth hearing.

You do not develop a friendly personality by telling funny stories. Listen attentively to others, but refuse to retaliate.

Remember names

We all like a man who remembers our name. We dislike the person who mispronounces our name, and we have little regard for anyone who calls us Mr Er . . . or Mr Um . . .

Frank Case said, *I think it humanly impossible for anyone to think of his own name as a word of little importance.*

How proud the average person feels when a head waiter greets him by name. The housewife preens herself when, after one visit to a shop, the assistant remembers her name. A buyer reacts in the same way.

Here is an approach that a salesman might make:

'Good morning, Mr Johnson, it is good of you to spare me your time. This is how we can cut down waste, Mr Johnson—just look at this . . .'

Read that aloud. Read it again, but this time leave out Mr Johnson's name. It doesn't sound the same, does it?

Here are some rules to guide you in remembering names:

1. You cannot remember a man's name if you are more interested in what you have to say than in what the buyer wants to hear. Be interested in him. Think of him as a personality. If you *want* to remember his name, you will.

2. After leaving a buyer, or anyone who can help you to get an order, write down their names. Refer to your diary every time you call on those people so that you get their names right.

3. Make certain that you know how to spell a name. When you ask a receptionist for a buyer's name, don't be satisfied with a gabbled answer. McPherson could sound just like Mackeson, Lemm could sound like Lamb. Ask the receptionist to spell the name and then spell it back, to make sure that you have it correctly.

4. Use the buyer's name during the sales presentation. Repetition will help to fix it firmly in your memory.

Tact

'No man with prejudices should ever be sent abroad to sell.' These words were used by an export director, who went on to explain that anyone with racial or religious prejudices would inevitably reveal them at some time or another, and thus lose orders and, more important, goodwill.

To the prejudiced, little advice can be given. They must cope as well as they can with their mixed-up outlook. To the unimaginative, little help can be given. If a man does not know he is doing wrong, how can he be cured of his faults? But most of us can learn to be more tactful.

Here are a few rules:

Men of all nationalities, colours, and creeds, can tell stories against themselves and enjoy them. They do not, however, relish the stories by others about their so-called characteristics.

Never make sweeping statements such as, 'I can't stand Frenchmen', or 'Italians get me down', or, 'The Swiss are a pain in the neck!' You may have disliked an Indian you have met or, perhaps, a Dutchman has annoyed you, but only a fool would condemn a whole nation because he disapproved of one or two of its people.

Do you want to know whether you are tactless? Ask yourself if you have ever greeted anyone with: 'You're not looking too well!' If so—you're tactless!

Giving Praise

Flattery is no part of a friendly personality. No one wants a friend who always lies—and to flatter is to lie. Buyers see through flattery, know it is false, and are not misled.

On the other hand, few people give praise and appreciation where it is due. The managing director won't praise his executive team—the executive team won't praise the office manager—the manager won't praise the staff—and the staff won't praise anyone. Too many sales managers find it easier to criticise a salesman than to praise him, and many a salesman would rather blow his own trumpet than raise the self-esteem of a buyer by praising his factory layout.

Those who complain bitterly that no one appreciates their efforts are often the very people who do not give praise in return.

How often have you heard such remarks as:

'He doesn't appreciate me!'

'They don't appreciate me!'

'They don't know what I do for them.'

'They're never satisfied.'

'You can kill yourself for him before you get a word of praise!'

'He's always grousing, but never gives anyone a pat on the back.'

These phrases are typical of people starved of praise. How do you react when someone praises you for work well done? Do you feel annoyed? Do you lose your temper with them? Of course not! You feel all the better for their kind words.

Constant criticism kills ambition, but praise boosts a man's self esteem, and everyone needs to feel important.

Look and See

How observant are you? Many people look, but see little. The flicker passing across a face when something distasteful has been said—the change of expression in a waiter's face when some buffoon snaps his fingers to attract his attention—the fear in a child's eyes as adults mention gruesome details of an illness—the glint of anger at some tactless remark—the attempt at bonhomie as a disguise for anxiety . . .

Only observant men notice these signs and tread warily by changing the topic of conversation, or by giving help where it is needed. It is a standard joke that no husband ever notices his wife's new hat or hair style. How many family quarrels have been caused by such a failure of observation? Women are usually much more observant than men. Men should strive for more equality of the sexes in this respect.

A Sincere Personality

To search our own souls and find that we have not been motivated by jealousy, envy, or unkindness, and that we have acted with sincerity is, indeed, a great satisfaction. Sincerity means being genuine, free from prejudice, the same in reality as in appearance. To look sad on hearing bad news but to be secretly delighted at another's misfortune is the height of insincerity. Both to appear and to be concerned is to be sincere. For a sincere personality you must pursue the ideal—you must be different from others, who are insincere without knowing it.

There is no excuse for a salesman who breaks his word. If there is an urgent reason for not keeping a promise—illness, perhaps—then the buyer should be telephoned immediately and told what has happened. In selling there is no substitute for dependability.

To be sincere you must keep all your promises, both big and small.

If a salesman cannot be loyal to his firm he should leave it. If a sales manager cannot be loyal to his salesmen he should be dismissed. It is not disloyal to leave a company for better terms and conditions elsewhere. Loyalty does not bind you to one company for ever. But so long as you are employed by a company you must give it your whole loyalty.

Be a Good Listener

Most of us talk too much. We think our own conversation so interesting and we know the other fellow's by heart.

Will Rogers said, *A good listener is not only popular everywhere, but after a while he knows something*. When you listen to your buyers instead of talking all the time you often learn a great deal.

What kind of a talker are you? Do you know that you may talk too much? If you don't realise this you may become a compulsive talker.

Are you a pouncer? In other words, do you rarely allow anyone to complete a story? You may be with a friend who is telling you his holiday experiences. He begins, 'I went to a travel agency to book for . . .' Without letting him finish you interrupt to tell him, 'You should have gone to Boon's, they're the best agents I know. When we went to Italy last year . . .'

Then there is the health pouncer. You say to a friend, 'How are you?' He starts to reply, 'Not too well I'm afraid, I've got . . .' but you interrupt him with, 'Do you know when I got up this morning the pain in my back was so bad I just don't know how I carried on.'

Perhaps you have decided that you are not a pouncer. If so, are you a pouncer-capper? He not only interrupts, but caps every story. Perhaps someone says, 'We went out last evening and had a delightful meal.' Before he can tell you where he had the meal or what he ate you are eagerly telling him, 'You should try Blotto's one day; they serve a six-course dinner with wine, and all the film stars go there. The other day I saw . . .'

Don't be a pouncer. Don't be a pouncer-capper. Sincere men

are good listeners; they are sincerely interested in other people. When the other person is talking, never, by gesture or expression, indicate that you are eager to say your piece. Look as if you are interested and listening. Don't let your eyes wander round the room. Nothing is more annoying than to know that a listener is only pretending to listen. You may be telling someone in a hotel lounge what is, to you, a most interesting story. Suddenly you realise that he is not listening, but is following the movements of everyone passing through the swing doors. He is not even paying you the compliment of pretending to be interested in your story.

Develop the habit of being an *intent* listener.

Four into One

For a selling personality you must combine four personalities. Here they are again:

a cheerful personality;
a strong personality;
a friendly personality;
a sincere personality.

This chapter has had two aims: The first is to clarify the selling personality; and the second is to convince you that one of a salesman's greatest assets is a knowledge of human relations.

Can one live up to this precept? I doubt it. Only a saint could follow all the advice in this chapter, but we can aim for perfection, although we may fall short.

Perhaps we cannot smile all the time. There are times when we lose our tempers, or make tactless remarks. We cannot always listen, listen, listen, or always refrain from criticism.

But we must constantly try to improve our human relations. As we succeed, we mould ourselves into professional salesmen.

Index

ABC OF SELLING, 121
adverse conditions for sales, 123–9
advice, asking for, 226
alternative close, 153–4, 201
apparent agreement technique for handling objections, 177
appointments by telephone, 70–81, 201–2
armchair planners, 85–6
attention, gaining, 115–17, 118, 122–44

BENEFITS OF PRODUCTS, 68–9, 92–109, 113, 119
proving, 149–50
blanket orders, 32
bluffers (buyers), 51–3
bonuses, 208
British Leyland Motor Corporation, 9
brush-off objections, 165–6
Bucky table, offer analysis sheet for, 108–9 (Fig. D)
busy buyers, 53
buy/make decision, 33, 37, 38
buyers
    adverse conditions created by, 124–9
    gaining attention of, 115–17, 118, 122–44
    identifying, 26–41
    kinds of, 42–55
    motivation of, 56–69
    needs of, see needs
    objections to purchase by, 158–77
    views on salesmen, 200, 203, 208–9, 216–22

CALL-BACK OPENINGS, 141–4

calls on customers, 79–81
    calling back, 138–44
    first calls, 129–30
    objectives, 23–5
    planning, 82–8, 191–204
canteen, selling in, 125–7
Carlyle, Thomas, 89
Case, Frank, 227
cellulose wrapping films, selling points, 97–8
centrifugal pumps, selling points, 98
chat gap, 129
closing sales, 121, 145–57
company policy, knowledge of, 210–11
competitors
    beating, 93–5, 139
    helping, 145
    knowing, 211–12
complaints, see objections
concession close, 156–7
confidence building, 89–92, 119
constant planners, 83–4
control relays, selling points, 98
conversational selling, 117–18
corridor, selling in, 127–8
cost accounts department, 39
cost effectiveness of selling, 188–9
customers (see also buyers)
    calling on, see calls
    grading, 190–1
    knowing, 210
    service to, 21

DAILY PLANNERS, 86–7
Daily Telegraph, 9
delay objections, 166–7
demonstration opening, 137–8
demonstration units, 87–8

dependability, 230
design department, 29–30, 33, 37–40
development calls, 138–44
directors, 43–6
double benefits, 92–3
Dunlop Company, 116

EMOTIONAL BUYING, 59–60
entertaining, 46–8
enthusiasm, 50, 208
estimating department, 39

FACTUAL OPENINGS, 131–2, 137, 141
'feeling' buyers, 43
first calls, 129–30
flattery, avoiding, 229–30
Fleming, Ian, 83
Ford Motor Company, 9
fork lift trucks, selling points, 96–7
forms handling equipment, selling points, 99
funny stories, avoiding, 227

GABBLING, 123
go-betweens, 27
goodwill, maintaining, 139
grading customers, 190–1

HANDSHAKING, 218–20
hidden objections, 168–70
hinges for interviews, 73–4
hotels, selling to, 178–80
human relations, 215–23

INCENTIVES, 208
industrial perfumes, offer analysis sheet for, 102–3 (Fig. B)
industrial salesmen, see salesmen
industrial selling, importance to the community, 10–11
inert gas system, selling points, 99
influential people, identifying, 27–8
information-seeking objections, 158
insulting openings, 123–4
interest, gaining, 115–17, 118, 122–44

interruption
    as selling technique, 48
    avoiding, when handling objections, 176
interviews
    hinges for, 73–4
    obtaining, 70–81
'intuitive' buyer, 43
investment, as sales benefit, 119

JAMES, WILLIAM, 224
Jung, Carl, 42

KEY SENTENCES, 115–17
knowledge
    acquisition of, 208–12
    of competitors, 211–12
    of customers, 210
    of product, 209–10

LEVENE, ROBERT, 187
link openings, 142–4
listening, importance of, 148–9, 231–2
loyalty
    by buyers, 173–6
    by salesmen, 231

MAKE/BUY DECISION, 33, 37, 38
management by objectives, 22
managing directors, 43–6
mannerisms, 222–3
manufacturing organisations, structure of, 29–41
    chart, 36
markets, study of, 86
material control, 31–2, 34
memory, importance of, 112–15, 227–8
mental attitudes of salesmen, 213–15
meticulous planners, 83
milling machines, selling points, 98–9
minor point, closing on, 155
mistakes, admitting, 225–6
modular time planning, 195–6
Moss, Brian, 178

motivation of buyers, 56–69

NAMES, REMEMBERING, 227–8
needs of prospective customers
    filling, 65
    finding, 119
    unrecognised or real, 66–8, 161
new products, launching, 20–1
newspapers, as sources of planning
    information, 85–6
Nu-aire (Contracts) Ltd., 27, 67–8,
    178

OBJECTIONS TO PURCHASE
    analysing, 160–76
    forestalling, 162–5
    overcoming, 24–5, 158–77
objectives, selling by, 22–5
offer analysis, 89–109
    sheets, 99–109
opening sales, 112–5, 121, 122–44
optimism, 214–15
orders, steps to, 118–21, 150–3
organisational structure, 29–41
    chart, 36
out and home sales route, 197
over-friendly buyers, 49

PARDOE, TERRY, 27
patents, 18
peripheral (petal) sales routes, 197
    (Fig. 3), 198
personality, 223–32
Personnel Hygiene Services Ltd., 42
persuasion, when selling, 15–19
'petal' sales routes, 197 (Fig. 3),
    198
planning calls on customers, 82–8,
    191–204
praise, importance of, 229–30
pre-call planning, 83–8
prejudices, avoiding, 228–9
price
    introducing, 172–3
    objection by buyers, 170–2
pride, buyer motivation, 59
primary objections to purchase,
    160–1

problem-solving motivators, 61–3
products
    analysing, 92–3
    benefits, see benefits
    knowing, 209–10
production control department,
    31–2, 34
production engineering depart-
    ment, 30–1, 33, 37–40
profession, definition of, 205–6
professional salesmen, characteris-
    tics of, 205–32
professional standards, 206–8
prospecting, 79–81
purchasing department, 32–5,
    38–42

QUESTION OPENINGS, 132–4, 137, 142

RANK XEROX, 66
rational motives for buying, 60–1
real (unrecognised) needs, 66–8,
    161
receptionists, treatment of, 80–1
reference openings, 134–5, 142
reminders, 85
re-order point, 32
repeat orders, 32
Rogers, Will, 148, 231
Rover cars, 60

SALES
    aids, as openings, 206–7
    closing, 121, 145–57
    costs, 188–9
    department, 29
    forecasting, 31
    kits, 87–8
    openings, 112–15, 121, 122–44
    specifications, 29
    territories, 187–204
Salesmanship (magazine), 206–7
salesmen
    adverse conditions created by,
        123–4
    appearance of, 217–18
    buyers' views of, 200, 203, 208–9,
        216–22

salesmen – *cont.*
  human relations of, 215–23
  importance of, 7–13
  influencing power of, 14–21
  professional characteristics of, 205–32
scared buyers, 49–50
selective objections, 161–2
selling
  ABC of, 121
  by objectives, 22–5
  points, 96–109
semi-planners, 84
sentences
  insulting, 123–4
  key, 115–7
sentiment, buyer motivation, 59–60
shop floor selling, 124–5
sincerity, 230–1
smoking, 220–2
specifying authorities, 178–86
standards, professional, 206–8
steps to orders, 118–21, 150–3
stock control, 31–2, 34
Stokoe, Bob, 211
stubborn buyers, 53
summary close, 154–5
suppliers
  selection, 33
  vetting, 34

TACITURN BUYERS, 50–1
Tack key sentence, 115–16
Tack Organisation, 22, 27, 120
Tack Research Ltd., 187
Tack surveys
  buyers' views on salesmen, 200, 203, 208–9, 216–22
  entertaining, 48

tact, importance of, 228–9
talkative buyers, 48–9
talking, pitfalls of, 148
Talleyrand, 168
target setting, 22
telephone appointments, 70–81, 201–2
territory planning, 187–204
'thinking' buyers, 42
Thixofix, 116–17
time, planning, 191–204
timid buyers, 49–50
too-friendly buyers, 49
trial close, 155
trust, importance of, 185–6

'UNMENTIONABLE' BUYERS, 46
unrecognised needs, 66–8, 161

VETTING SUPPLIERS, 34, 39
visiting cards, 79–80
visits by customers, arranging 23–4

WANTS, CREATING, 63–5
washer extractor, offer analysis sheet for, 104–7 (Fig. C)
water treatment, offer analysis sheet for, 101 (Fig. A)
weekly planning, 85–6
weekly time cycles, 192–7
words, use of, 110–18
work study, 30–1

X-RAY EQUIPMENT, OFFER ANALYSIS SHEET FOR, 108–9 (Fig. D)

YOU APPEAL, 96–109, 116, 149–50, 162

Other CEDAR titles . . .

Dale Alexander
The New Arthritis and Common Sense   434 01819 8

Yvonne Allen
Successfully Single, Successfully Yourself   434 11155 4

Thérèse Bertherat & Carol Bernstein
The Body Has Its Reasons   434 11138 4

Frank Bettger
How I Multiplied My Income & Happiness in Selling   434 11108 2
How I Raised Myself from Failure to Success in Selling 434 11159 7

Judith Brown
I Only Want What's Best for You   434 11137 6

Dale Carnegie
How to Develop Self-Confidence and Influence
  People by Public Speaking   434 11153 8
How to Enjoy Your Life and Your Job   434 11160 0
How to Stop Worrying and Start Living   434 11130 9
How to Win Friends and Influence People   434 11119 8
The Quick and Easy Way to Effective Speaking   434 11152 X

Samuel H. Klarreich
The Stress Solution   434 11158 9

Robert & Marilyn Kriegel
The C Zone – Peak Performance Under Pressure   434 11121 X

Mildred Newman & Bernard Berkowitz
How to Be Your Own Best Friend   434 11154 6

Norman Vincent Peale
The Amazing Results of Positive Thinking   434 11117 1
Enthusiasm Makes the Difference   434 11136 8
A Guide to Confident Living   434 11128 7
Inspiring Messages for Daily Living   434 11107 4
The Joy of Positive Living   437 95168 5
The New Art of Living   434 11120 1
The Positive Principle Today   434 11112 0
Positive Thoughts for the Day   434 11123 6
The Positive Way to Change Your Life   434 11129 5
Power of the Plus Factor   434 11139 2
The Power of Positive Thinking   434 11116 3
The Power of Positive Thinking for Young People   434 11118 X
Stay Alive All Your Life   434 11115 5
The Tough Minded Optimist   434 11135 X
Unlock Your Faith-Power   434 11113 9
You Can If You Think You Can   434 11124 4

Norman Vincent Peale & Smiley Blanton
The Art of Real Happiness   434 11127 9
Faith Is The Answer   437 95012 5

Dr Charles Shepherd
Living With M.E.   434 11156 2

Alfred Tack
Building, Training and Motivating a Sales Force   437 95159 6
How to Increase Your Sales to Industry   434 11126 0
How to Increase Your Sales by Telephone   434 11111 2
How to Overcome Nervous Tension and Speak Well
  in Public   434 11106 6
How to Succeed as a Sales Manager   434 11110 4
How to Succeed in Selling   434 11125 2
Marketing: The Sales Manager's Role   437 95156 1
1000 Ways to Increase Your Sales   434 11132 5

Judith Tatelbaum
The Courage to Grieve   434 11105 3

Denis Waitley
Seeds of Greatness   434 11122 8

G. Kingsley Ward
Letters of a Businessman to His Son   434 11157 0

For further information on how to obtain
Cedar books, please contact the publisher:

William Heinemann Ltd,
Michelin House,
81 Fulham Road,
London SW3 6RB

The
TACK ORGANISATION

is the largest training organisation of its kind in the world. It has twelve thousand client companies in the United Kingdom including many leading names in industry and commerce. Companies in the TACK group market products and services through every type of outlet and provide the up-to-date practical experience on which all training is based.

This practically, together with highly professional teaching methods, has largely accounted for the success and growth of the Training Division, which offers these courses:

■ **FINANCE**
Finance for the Senior Executive
Introduction to Finance for Managers
Cash Collection and Credit Control
Intoduction to International Commerce

■ **MANAGEMENT AND SUPERVISORY**
Leadership in Senior Management
The Multi-Discipline Manager
Executive Development
Communication and Negotiation Skills for Managers
Motivational Leadership
Effective Supervision
Effective Supervision – Part 2
Effective Office Management
Effective Office Management – Part 2
Profitable Time Management
Executive Decision Making
Recruitment Interviewing and Selection
Performance Appraisal

■ **COMMUNICATION**
Effective Speaking
Effective Report Writing
Better Letter Writing
Better Use of the Telephone

■ **SALES**
Sales Training
Sales Training – Part 2
Selling to Industry
Selling to Industry – Part 2
Professional Sales Development
Profitable Negotiating
Professional Telephone Selling
Dealing with Customers by Telephone
Successful Territory Management
Selling to Wholesalers and Retailers
Selling Financial Services
Better Selling through Financial Awareness

■ **MARKETING AND SALES MANAGEMENT**
Field Sales Management
Field Sales Management - Part 2
Profitable Sales Management
Introduction to Marketing

■ **SPECIALIST TRAINING**
Caring for the Customer
Customer Relations for Service Engineers
The Executive Secretary
Introduction to Microcomputers
Training the Trainer

In-Company Training is provided in all these areas, specially designed to suit specific client requirements.

Open Courses are run regularly on most of the above topics, with mixed attendance by client companies from all areas of industry and commerce.

THE TACK ORGANISATION
LONGMOORE STREET LONDON SW1V 1JJ

Telephone 01-834-5001